THE Fearless AGENT

A Manual for Real Estate Success
Book 1

IVANIA ALVARADO

*Everything You Need to Know to Start (or Improve) Your Real Estate Business
Plus 90-Day Undated Action Planner*

Business basics, mindset training, and simple guidance
to achieve your desired real estate success.

Use this book to prepare the ground for sowing and reaping
the fruits of success that will last forever.

Contents

Introduction

This manual shares the steps you can take as a new (or recommitted) real estate agent, so you can experience resounding success in your national and international profession. It's an excellent guide for new agents who are just starting out, as well as agents with experience who want a 180-degree change in their life and business. New agents will gain vast experience and knowledge, while brokers can use this guide to assist their agents in breaking through current income ceilings.

The qualities I suggest agents adopt and the teachings I describe will show readers a proven path to success. In this manual, I recommend theories and practices brokers can encourage their agents to use with the company as a study guide.

After doing several studies, I have noticed only a very small percentage of agents make money in this business. Have you ever wondered why? So many people get their licenses but don't earn a check or remain an agent. In fact, in the real estate business, some people spend years as agents without receiving a single check. That makes me sad and worried for them. If you're an agent who doesn't earn money but needs to, you likely don't have the tools you need to succeed. You've invested time and money in being a real estate agent for some reason, and that reason is still important to you.

One of the biggest reasons an agent does not invest in their own education is because they do not know what kind of agent they are now and what type of agent they want to be. You need to know yourself first so you can develop the right habits to reach your goals. Start your business on the right foot.

There are several types of agents in this book that I will mention, but right now I want to mention two:

1. The agent who lives for the real estate business.
2. The agent whose real estate business lives for them.

Who are you today?

When you ask yourself this question, decide which answer you prefer. Furthermore, every time you ask a question, decide if it's better to act or to *think* before you act.

Chapter 1

How Do I Get Started?

Humility vs the Ego

This question is very important. Start like a first grader. Be present for every moment in which you're studying. With this manual, you will learn things that will lead you to success immediately if you study and apply the knowledge you learn.

When you were a child, you learned new information faster and you absorbed everything like a sponge that is thirsty for spilled liquid. Your ego let you learn quickly and easily. When you grew up and became an adult, your ego grew drastically too. It stayed with you and allowed you to speak your fears. Your ego tells you and others what you know and the effort you are making to grow and improve. This will raise the following questions: With all this learning and growing, why am I not where I want to be? Why don't things go the way I want them to? Even more so, I do the same things that the star agent does who earns six figures, yet I don't. Why did he?

Your ego fills you with expectations. These expectations can make it difficult for you to learn new habits and information. For example, if a glass is full of any liquid, it will overflow if another drop is added to it. You must empty the glass as much as you can to add the liquid you *want* to drink. When you study this manual, you will have to do the same. As you read, set your own knowledge aside so you can absorb new information. When you learn the new information, subconsciously and unconsciously you will create new habits and disciplines. Then you can put the old knowledge and new knowledge together, pick out the best parts, and create an "atomic bomb" of prosperity in your favor.

Switch from the Inside Out

To succeed, you must make a change in your life. That is only achieved by making a change on the inside. Obviously, if you continue to do the same thing, you will have the same results. You have proven this for years, and you know you're not satisfied with the results.

How do you change? It's very easy. I will repeat this constantly. **It's very easy. Tell your brain it is possible, and it is easy to change** if you **believe it.**

Make a habit of repeating these affirmations every day:

1. **The real estate business is easy and effective.**
2. **I am a multimillion-dollar producer.**
3. **Everyone wants to buy and sell their properties with me.**
4. **I have abundant wealth.**

Change your habits in your real estate business from passive to active.

Example

Agent 1: Says he/she is a full-time agent.

The agent arrives at the office almost every day and stays there for at least four hours minimum. He/she chats all the time, uses the computer, checks email, goes to lunch, and reads posts on social media. He/she talks to a prospective buyer, looks for some properties without prequalifying the buyer beforehand, and wastes time with customers without knowing if they qualify for what they want to buy. The agent ends the day exhausted, finally arriving home, and hasn't closed any real estate for more than six months. The agent becomes frustrated with the business, assumes the real estate business is bad, and assumes the economy is bad too.

The agent needs to change their bad habits by taking responsibility for them, then put new, better habits into place.

The same agent:

Arrives at the office at 9:00 am. The first thing the agent does is put up an "I Am Busy" sign that asks they not be interrupted from 9:00-10:00 a.m. The agent uses this blocked time to call customers and prospects to book appointments. The first, most important thing the agent can do for the business is prospecting.

This is the time to move from passive to active agent and respect your time, money, and business. To create positive change from the inside out, recognize what you are doing wrong and be able to change it. Get to the root of the problem and take immediate action; if you do not do this quickly, you'll fall into the same vicious cycle. This is one of the reasons agents fail in this business, not because of the economy, customers, or banks. This bad habit is like any other bad habit or addiction and should be treated in the same way.

If you work at home, put the same "Do Not Disturb" sign on your desk so your partner, children, and family members respect that you are working. You must give yourself the respect first.

Create Solid, Deep Foundations Like an Oak Tree

Whether you're in real estate or any other business, you must create solid foundations. Don't wait to start your business until after you acquire the knowledge you need. Instead, use this manual as theory and practice at the same time. Learn then act. The real estate business is a business of action; only those who have training and then act on it are successful. Apply what you learn. Application is a requirement for success. You CAN become a multimillionaire agent who lives from the proceeds of your business. You deserve it.

What are the basics?

- Having self-discipline
- Being a good boss
- Firing yourself if necessary and re-employing yourself after you make changes to your business and habits
- Sticking to your action plan, and your short-, medium-, and long-term goals
- Paying attention to social relationships
- Making social media posts and interacting with leads
- Doing the "Full Circle" (explained in the next section) over and over with each client
- Creating your database and working on it
- Building more followers on social media who become prospects and future clients (is your social media effective?)

- Learning something new every day, or every week at least
- Acting today in your present; tomorrow is not promised
- Respecting your time as if you are at a full-time job that you can't leave whenever you want or to do something for your family
- Knowing your target market
- Being self-motivated (create your daily self-management system you can use whenever you are down or for whatever reason)
- Creating your own powerful mantra in moments of need such as a listing presentation, when you are drained, or when you are low in energy to help you get out of fear and negativity.

Real Estate Full Circle

The "Full Circle" is essential for the long life of your business. You will do the full circle with each client. It consists of four steps: **1. Schedule the appointment, 2. Do the presentation, 3. Contract-Sell-Close 4. Ask for references.** Repeat the cycle with each client to gain a much better clientele. If you do this, every year you will multiply your customers, resulting in multiplied revenue.

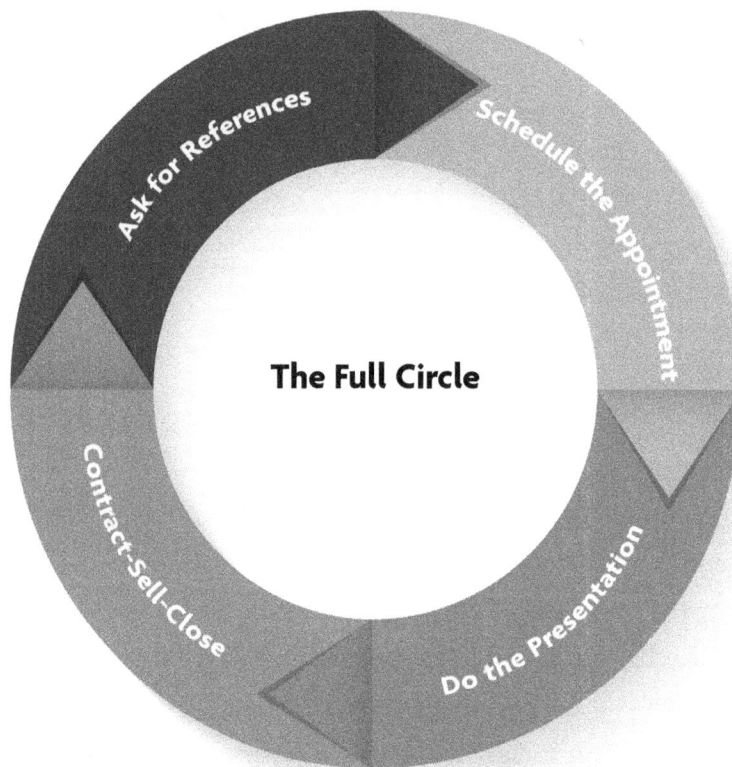

The Full Circle

Ask for References

Schedule the Appointment

Do the Presentation

Contract-Sell-Close

For example, if you start the circle and work with three new customers in one month, you will ask for three to five referrals from each customer, resulting in nine to fifteen new leads who could be potential buyers, sellers, tenants, or landlords in a single month. Imagine you do the same thing repeatedly over the course of a year. That would be a gain of 90-150 leads, assuming you take two months off for vacation. *If you perfect the entire circle by working the referrals, this may be the only thing you need to do for prospecting.

Act

As established before, the real estate business is built on action. It is not a business that waits for clients to come through the door, unless you work as a home developer, condominium owner, or a property management company. If that's not your scenario, you should plan on taking proactive steps to reach out to new clients for at least two hours every day.

Cleaning and Organization

Cleaning and organization are essential to attract success. Start with your home, then your car, and finally your office or business.

You might think, "But I want to make money, not organize and clean my house." I encourage you to create a place in your home that is dedicated to work. This will be just for you. It's critical you pick a place where no one disturbs you and you are at peace, with a pleasant work area that inspires you, that smells clean and is well-organized. You should know where everything is and have all the necessary office equipment, such as the internet, your computer, a printer, a place to record information, stationery, folders, and anything else you might need. You will spend most of your working hours in this location, and the environment you create is of paramount importance to your accomplishment.

Your car is another important element for your success as a real estate agent. You will spend a great deal of your time in the car driving and you cannot miss any chances by having a messy car. Your car is your office. Create an area on the side of the trunk by placing a divider there, then put your contracts and stationery, advertisements, cards, doorhangers, lockboxes, and signs in that spot. You may also have an FSBO (For Sale by Owner) advertisement, flyer, or postcard to offer the owner of an FSBO. Have blank contracts of all kinds for when you have a spur of the moment customer. You don't want to miss a sale because you don't have the right kind of paperwork available when you need it. Keep your business cards and any type of postcards, flyers, or advertising that you will need to hand out. This says you are an active agent who is always readily available to help new clients.

In your email system, keep a folder handy that contains sample contracts: for listings, tenants, and buyers. In cases when you don't have access to the MLS or other listings, you'll be able to email a contract to your client immediately. It's even possible to edit a Word doc on your phone, save it to PDF, then email it to your client right there on the spot. Keep the Word doc prefilled with your own information and company information, so all you need to do is enter the client and price details on the contract. You can also buy a Transaction Manager system to organize your contracts inside your backoffice and tasks. Recommended software includes Total Brokerage, DotLoop, BrokerMint, KvCore, and LionDesk for CRM.

Finally, tidy your office desk. You should have everything mentioned above readily available to attract and assist potential customers.

What Kind of Agent Are You?

You should know yourself well enough to understand the way you will react and respond in your professional field.

- How important is it for you to succeed?
- Are you the kind of person who lets others train you?
- Do you know how to delegate?
- Do you know your talents, virtues, strengths, and weaknesses?
- What you do well? What don't you do well?
- What do you like the most about the real estate business? What do you like the least?
- What would you be willing to do to increase your income? What would you never do?

Knowing yourself well will help you reach your real estate goals faster. Working on your strongest skills and delegating what you do not like to do will help you have better results.

What kind of partner would be the most appropriate for your business? Your best partner should be someone you like, but more importantly your partner should be someone who brings the skills you do not already have into your business. They should complement your efforts.

Start asking yourself what you do not like to do, as it will help you adapt to the pros and cons of the real estate business.

Self-Assessment Questionnaire:

What do you dislike the most about your real estate business?

_____

_____

_____

What would you never be willing to do for your business?

_____

_____

_____

Which business skills do you lack the most? What is the hardest work for you to do?

_____

_____

_____

Are there any tasks you don't like to do, but you do them anyway because you know they are necessary?

_____

_____

_____

What would you like to learn from this business? What would you prefer NOT to learn?

_____

_____

_____

Do you have any habits that you would prefer not to change even if doing so would improve your career?

_____

_____

_____

What do you like the most about this business?

_____

_____

_____

What would you be willing to do for your business?

_____

_____

_____

What would you like to learn to increase your income and/or customers?

_____

_____

_____

What negative habit would you be willing to change in your business so you can be more positive and productive?

_____

_____

_____

What are you good at? What do you do better than most?

_____

_____

_____

What are your best qualities?

_____

_____

_____

What characteristics might a partner have that you would never want to associate with or hire because they would not suit your success plan or business?

_____

_____

_____

Why did you start in the real estate business?

_____

_____

_____

What's your reason for doing this business? What's your big WHY? Enumerate each of the reasons:

_____

_____

_____

_____

*Knowing why and your reasons are two questions with the same meaning. When asked in a different way, they may reach your subconscious and get a more genuine response. The why is important so you know what moves you and what turns you on in this business. When you become discouraged for whatever reason by any customer, the economy, or an unexpected setback, you will remember why you started this business.

What do you want to get out of this business?

_____

_____

_____

What characteristics and qualities would you look for in someone before you hired or partnered with them in your business for your growth?

_____

_____

_____

Write a summary of the type of agent you think you are after you answer each question. Read each of your responses and do a self-assessment. This type of deep self-assessment will reveal the type of agent you are. The answer is in your heart.

_____

_____

_____

_____

_____

_____

Now write what you promise to improve in yourself so you can do better in your business:

_____

_____

_____

_____

_____

What habits will you change and replace with new, healthier habits?

_____

_____

_____

_____

_____

Now that you know what kind of agent you are, you know if you want to stay the same or make changes. You also know the qualities you're looking for in a partner and why they're important to have as part of the team.

What Kind of Agent Do You Want to Become?

When you have answered the questionnaire honestly, you will realize the type of real estate agent or seller you are and want to become. You will also be able to recognize the root of the problem and the perfect remedy to fix it. Now you know the type of partner you need to make the perfect team, instead of the friend or partner you have, unless that person already has the needed characteristics.

Now that you know the type of agent you want to become, focus on the qualities this future agent has as if you are already that person. Make that your reality today.

The agent you were in the past is not the agent you are now or will be in the future. Your present is what you project from now on, today. Your present is, "I am a/n _____ agent." (Finish your sentence with the type of agent you declare you are now.)

Do the affirmation exercise aloud so you not only read it and memorize it, but also listen to it. The tongue accelerates the process of change and tells the brain what to do. The universe will bring these things to you by your intention. The tongue is the most important organ because it allows you to connect with your brain and attract what you say. When you affirm a statement, you help that statement become a reality. Almost everything you constantly repeat will come true, so be careful with what you say. Your tongue is like a magic wand.

For example:

- I, _____, am an agent who sells __#__ million dollars every year.
- I, _____, am a top producing agent.
- I, _____, close/sell five transactions every month.
- I, _____, am the best salesperson of the year in my company.

You can add what you want to your repetitions. You can also create new positive habits through repetitions.

For example:

- I love to do telemarketing.
- I, _____, am a champion at making appointments.
- I, _____, am an organized person
- I, _____, love to work on my social media.
- I, _____, post every day on my social media channels to attract new leads and followers.

You must also believe the statements you make. Behave with the attitude of the person who is completing these goals and, above all, act.

You will have bigger and faster results if you visualize your goals as you repeat your affirmations. Repeat the statement and see the result in your mind.

Keep your communication positive, and try to talk only with productive, positive people. Read about personal improvement and avoid talking about problems. Focus. Think, act, visualize, feel, and repeat your affirmations. Declare what you are already from this moment on.

Stay busy because you have a lot to do. The 80/20 rule states that 80% of the day's results are due to what you think and 20% are what you do. If you think positively and visualize what you want, you will get results.

You likely spend more time thinking than doing, so be sure to use this rule in your favor. You want every opportunity to move faster. It's catastrophic if you use it against yourself. Avoid overthinking your problems and difficulties; be very careful about what you're thinking and don't sabotage your success.

Image and Profile

Clothing is another important factor. You sell yourself and your image, as well as professionalism, service, and knowledge. Keep that in mind, especially when you go to a listing presentation to sell someone's house. Remember, you only have one chance to make a first impression. After all, if you make a poor first impression, there may never be a second one. This is so important that companies or individuals will pay a consultant to teach them how to dress like a professional who makes millions. They want to project themselves as successful to improve their self-esteem and confidence.

Evaluate Your Beliefs

Your beliefs can help or harm you. Take the following test to find out if your beliefs could be your best allies or your worst enemies. If you find your beliefs are your worst enemies, you will need to analyze which of your beliefs is affecting your personal growth. You'll want to eliminate it immediately and **create new and more powerful beliefs** that will be with you on your journey to success.

Belief Questionnaire:

1. Do you think having more money will hurt you? Yes____ NO____ If yes, why you think having more money will hurt you?

   _____

   _____

2. Do you think working hard is harmful to your family? Yes____ NO____ Why?

   _____

   _____

3. Do you think money is bad or does it change people? Yes____ NO____ Why do you think that? Provide examples.

   _____

   _____

   _____

4. Are you afraid of success? Yes____ NO____ Why?

   _____

   _____

5. Do you think people who have money aren't good people? Yes____ NO____ Why?

   _____

   _____

6. Has anyone ever told you that money is bad or that it changes people? Yes____ NO____ Who?

   _____

   _____

7. Do you consider yourself a positive, optimistic, or negative person? Yes___ NO___ Why do you think you're this way? How does that show up in your life?

_____

_____

_____

8. Do you think you have to work hard or kill yourself with work to make money? Yes___ NO___ Why?

_____

_____

9. Do you think you have to speak English to be a successful realtor? Yes___ NO___ Why?

_____

_____

10. Do you think you should have a college degree to make more money? Yes___ NO___ Why?

_____

_____

11. Do you believe in yourself and the likelihood that you will be able to achieve everything you want? Yes___ NO___ Why?

_____

_____

12. Do you think you need your partner's support of your career to succeed in it? Yes___ NO___ Why?

_____

_____

13. Do you think if your partner, parents, or children don't support you, it's going to be more difficult for you than if they support you? Yes____ NO____ Why?

_____

_____

14. Do you think age is a problem or does it affect your business? Yes____ NO____ Why?

_____

_____

15. Do you think you need someone else to succeed or for someone to believe in you or for someone to support you? Yes____ NO____ Why?

_____

_____

16. Do you think you need to be in a stable relationship to succeed? Yes____ NO____ Why?

_____

_____

17. Do you think if your relationship with your partner goes wrong, that's why you're not doing well in your business? Yes____ NO____ Why?

_____

_____

18. Do you think your problems are the cause of how bad your business is? Yes____ NO____ Why?

_____

_____

19. Do you think the problem with your business is because of the economy or real estate regulation? Yes____ NO____ Why? And how this is the cause?

_____

_____

20. Do you want to make peace with money? Yes____ NO____ Why do you think is important to have peace with money and have a good relationship with wealth?

_____

_____

_____

_____

"If you are going to be successful in creating the life of your dreams, you have to believe that you are capable of making it happen."

-Jack Canfield

When you realize which of your beliefs are holding you back, toss them out and eliminate every belief that prevents you from either your growth or your economic increase. Only then can you achieve positive and effective change.

If you do not eliminate your negative beliefs, you will stay in the same spot. You will continue having a conflict between your goals and your beliefs and the belief that is the strongest will win. This is the time to say goodbye to negative beliefs once and for all.

Make peace with money and have a healthy relationship with it if you want to be successful; otherwise, you will continue to sabotage yourself. In your family, if their relationship with money was good, you will have a good relationship with money. If they didn't, it's likely you won't have success with money. For instance, if you believe money is bad, you won't be prosperous, because you will believe you must also be bad to become wealthy. Make peace with your relationship with money. People do many things they later regret to make money. You want it to work for you (rather than you doing anything or everything to work for it).

"You are a living magnet. What you attract into your life is in harmony with your dominant thoughts."

-Brian Tracy

The next exercise will help you visualize how to eliminate the things that no longer serve you.

Imagine you go into your closet. Observe how many clothes still occupy your closet even though you don't wear them anymore. Maybe they don't fit you, you don't like them, they're damaged, or have gone out of fashion. It is the same thing with your old negative beliefs or habits that have occupied a space in your mind but no longer belong there. These old negatives beliefs and habits have already become unfashionable. They no longer fit into current business trends and no longer fit your needs. Remove them to free up space for the new beliefs that will help you grow and improve your real estate career. Like clothing you no longer wear, take them out of your closet. When you do this, you'll be able to see the clothes that do fit and buy clothes that are more appropriate for the lifestyle you currently have.

Do not be afraid to throw out your old negative beliefs and bad habits or old-fashioned way of working. It is better to throw out the trash early instead of waiting until it rots and stinks. ***Do not let stagnancy take over your life.*** Successful people are constantly improving, changing, and adapting to new ways of working.

Chapter 2

Learn Something New Every Day

Go to Your Board/Association Classes

Take all the classes you can to stay updated on changing trends in the real estate industry. Check the calendar each month. If you have an assistant, some associations will allow your assistant to attend the classes, too. Give your assistant access to the MLS (Multiple Listing Service). The MLS is a database where you can search for all properties, comparables, listings of properties for sale, and more.

Take advantage of the resources that are offered to you. Become a member of Florida Realtors Rewards and the NAR (National Association of Realtors). These organizations offer members discounted rates at multiple companies such as: Office Depot, rent-a-car companies, hotels, cruise lines, insurance agencies, phone companies, banks, discounted credit cards, service companies, electronics, educational tools, and more.

Going to annual conferences will keep you updated with new programs, techniques, and strategies.

Take classes to certify and specialize in what you like and want to become: Accredited Buyer's Representative (ABR), Certified Residential Specialist (CRS), Short Sale and Foreclosure Resource Certification (SFR), Seniors Real Estate Specialist (SRES), Graduate, REALTOR® Institute (GRI), commercial, luxury (luxury properties), and more.

The associations offer many tools to their members that will support your business. You may not even know about all of them. Following is a list of some additional benefits you may want to use. Your association may have others or use different names. Here are several resources:

	AnnounceMyListing.com: To advertise listings/properties for sale
	ePropertyWatch.com: Information and news about the neighborhood
	inman.com: Breaking news, objective analysis, special reports, and more
	MiamiRealtors.com/commercial/member-2-member-marketing/: Member-to-member services in the commercial area
	MLSAdvantage: Share your MLS listings across Florida and more
	MyCondoPlans.com: Condo plans, house plans, listings, and more
	DataCo-op.com: Access properties for sale throughout the U.S. Search for properties in other associations (other MLS listings) in the nation
	Agent3000.com: Landing page, social media tools, website, and more

		Amarki.com: Complete marketing platform to send information to your contacts by email, text, or social networks with templates and information
		Realtor.com: Deep link information for agents
		ShowingTime.com: A service that helps agents and brokers make appointments to show properties from the MLS by scheduling showings, sending offers, and more
		Homes.com: Integrated platform to market and help manage your customers
		RETechnology.com: Comprehensive technology ratings resource for agents
		IDXBroker.com: Internet Data Exchange. Have the MLS on your website, including information about the local market
		NARRPR.com: Realtor property resource. Online real estate database
		GreatSchools.org: Reports, exams, and scores of private and/or public schools (from elementary to high school) in the area

	SupraeKey.com: Electronic security box, key, and configuration
	CoreLogic.com: MLS flexibility, functionality, and speed across all browsers and devices. Property search system, add, edit properties, check comparables, and more
	Remine.com: Search for MLS, tax, consumer information, and more
	Realdax.com: Pro-form-CMA market analytics
	FormSimplicity.com: Documents, real estate forms, contracts, e-sign, and more
	Realtor.com: NAR- National Agent Association. Resources for members. Numerous tools, events, benefits, discounts, and more
	MLSOffers.com: Hyperlink in MLS to send and receive offers, notifications about offers
	ListHub.com: National market network for realtors

		eCommission.com: Access to a commission advance
		EveryDoorDirectMail.com: Mail flyers and postcards door-to-door at lower prices
		iMapp.com: Comprehensive tax information and data tools by county
		DotLoop.com: Filling, negotiating, and electronically signing contracts
		WikiRealty.com: To grow and expand your network
		MyRental.com and LandlordStation.com: Tenant Record Report into MLS
		Realopedia.com: Global property listing, also to advertise your properties for customers and consumers in other countries
		RatePlug.com: Integrated with financial information on each property to calculate monthly payments and more

		SaleCore.com: IDX site, CRM, tools, and email marketing
		ListTrac.com: Measures user engagement data related to your properties for sale/listing
		RateMyAgent.com: Generate, share, promote and distribute customer reviews-MLS
		MiamiBrokerOpenHouse.com and SouthFloridaOpenHouseSearch. com: 24/7 Virtual tour, live and in-person open house.
		BuyDomainNamesandMore.com: Site to buy domain names
		ReboGateway.com: Rotation rates, local competition, and area rate
		WorldPropertyJournal.com: National and global real estate news. Great, current information to feed to your website
		Proxio.com: Global reference network and developer showcase

	BuildersUpdate.com and NewHomeSourceProfessional.com: Inventory of new properties under construction that are available in your area
	Sunstats.FloridaRealtors.org: Tool to view and create data, charts, reports by city and county
	HomeVisit.com: Photo, video, 3D, flat images, website for your property for sale, and direct mail
	BrokerCommand.com: Tools and reports for quick access to agent and office production
	CoreLogic.com: Property-focused tax reporting, data, and reports
	RealSatisfied.com: Simple tools to feed and publish your customers' recommendations.
	MiamiRealtorsLive.com: Pre-recorded and live classes from the realtor association
	Point2Homes.com/agent-websites/: Brokers panel for listing distribution

Your association may have training and informational videos on YouTube. Here is the training site from Miami Association of Realtors: miamire.com and channel: https://www.youtube.com/miamitrainers.

Attend Your Broker/Office Trainings

Attending all office trainings will help you stay connected and focused on your goals. Ask your broker for the office challenges and work towards the goals and recognition. These achievements will improve your resume and help you become a better sales associate.

Many companies publicize the best agent of the month, quarter, or year on the door of the office and on their company website and social media. This exposure will show your clients the type of agent you are, so use it in your favor when you interview them.

This is not about ego. It's quite the opposite, because what you must sell best is yourself, even before you sell a property, product, or service. Your customer wants to have a star agent, not a mediocre one. They also don't want to feel as if the only customer you have is them. They do not want to have the responsibility of knowing that if they don't buy from you, you will end up with nothing, or that you are experimenting with them because you have no experience.

Sellers want an agent with more experience and security. Sellers want agents who will sell their house quickly and at the highest possible price.

Keep Educating Yourself

Like all professionals, a doctor must continue studying new diseases, cures, and treatments. Real estate agents must continue their education too. There will always be new regulations, sales systems, technology changes, and ways to stay motivated. The key to this business is to keep your passion for it alive. Continuing education is one way to do this.

I recommend reading or listening to audios on topics that will help you in your career:

- Real estate, financing
- Motivation, self-esteem
- Sales and closing strategies, systems that generate customers, how to influence people, etc.

- Technology
- Social media techniques
- Image and projection
- Marketing
- Video and photography class
- Public speaking
- Website design
- How to create a blog
- Create and maintain a YouTube channel; how to use YouTube for marketing

Chapter 3

Socialize and Watch Your Income Multiply!

From an early age, some people know how to excel in their social relationships, while others do not. If you are already a charismatic person and it is easy for you to make friends by creating rapport with people, that's fabulous; if that is not the case, you will have to work on this skill. Having great social skills will help you have more customers and earn more money if you use them in your favor.

Optimize Your Business Card/E-Card

Having multiple business cards is ideal so you can have one card for each type of customer. What you put on the card depends on the type of customer you want to attract or work with more.

If you do not know what the person in front of you might be interested in, give them a generic, standard business card.

Agents need at least three different types of business cards:

1. A generic card you could give to anyone that starts with words like SELL-BUY-RENT, or whatever kind of business you want to attract first
2. A card to attract buyers and/or tenants
3. A card to attract sellers and/or landlords

If you want to attract *either* a seller or a buyer, have a customized card for each of them.

Example of a card to attract sellers:

Ivania Alvarado
Your house sold in 21 days or less!
Real Estate by Ivania
www.YourName.com
ivania@YourName.com
305-555-1234

- Buy a domain using your name as the URL to start branding your name. As a real estate professional, you sell yourself first.
- Change "21 days or less" to whatever timeline you prefer: 15 days, one week, or one month, whichever you prefer.
- Place all this information on the back of the card. (The front of the business card is for the name of your real estate company.) You can use this either for your general card or whichever customized card you're using.
- The websites used on the cards are just examples for how they might look. You could buy a domain for use exclusively in your work with sellers, buyers, landlords, and tenants, or use the same one you have for everyone using your own name to create branding.

Attention Sellers

How much is your house worth today?
The market is constantly changing.

www.Howmuchmyhouseworth.com

Exclusive for Buyers

Free list of properties in any area.
Auction, foreclosure, short sale. Receive detailed information about each property, price, number of bedrooms, address. www.encuentromicasa.com

Approaching People with Your Business Card and/or Material You Have Designed

- Start now to take advantage of your environment and hand out at least five business cards every day. You will need to remember to do this daily, to create discipline to become a habit. Soon, you will not be able to finish your day without doing it; it will be as ingrained a habit as brushing your teeth.

Some people start by handing out five business cards per day and develop their habit to reach fifteen to twenty people a day without having to pay advertising. They only need to reach out to the people they're in contact with in their everyday life. Their whole business depends in large part on handing out business cards, or any other type of advertising they have on hand. They will always find someone who is personally interested or who knows someone who will be. Just remember: the most important thing at first is to give cards away and take action.

- Add a QR code to your business card in case you only have one card on hand. The other person can just scan the code and can have all the information you would normally show on your card. Another option is to use an electronic business card that you can easily share with a client by putting your phone next to theirs.

If you do not have any type of advertisement with you, talk to people and exchange phone numbers, your web address, and your social media pages. When you have your own website, you can text the URL to a potential client. Your information will be there and on your social media business page. This makes it easier to connect with the prospect later.

Steps to approach people:

Start with the easiest people first. Next, approach anyone who is a meter (or three feet) away from you.

1. Start with anyone who is helping you, whether you are buying something or receiving a service from them, as these people should generally provide good service to the public, be kind, and take good care of you.
2. Whenever someone tells you they are interested in your service, whether it is to buy, sell, rent, or whatever, always ask for their phone number. Don't expect them to call you, as you are the one who is interested. You are the one who makes a living in this business.
3. Approach the cashier where you shop: the supermarket, a department store, etc.

4. Remember to include your child's teacher and other school employees.
5. Other professional contacts might include bank tellers, your accountant, lawyers, secretaries or receptionists, your manicurist, your hairdresser(s), waiters or waitresses, etc.

Adapt the following example to your personality.

Example #1 Approaching prospects with a business card, and/or any available marketing materials

You—Hello, how are you?

Them—Good.

You—Nice to meet you, my name is _____.

Them—Nice to meet you.

You—I am a real estate professional in this area. Just in case you or someone you know is interested in buying, selling, or renting any property, this is my information (hand them the business card and/or flyer). Are you interested or is someone you know interested?

Them—Yes or no (wait and listen).

* If the answer is **NO:**

You—Good, thank you very much for listening to me. Please let me know if in the future you or someone you know might need my services.

*If **YES:**

You—May I have your phone number so we can communicate better? We can make an appointment to talk, or I could send you a free list of available properties. Your number is? ………
(Wait till he/she gives it to you).

Once they give their phone number to you, if there's time and they can talk, ask them some questions like:

What are you looking for?

What do you need?

From there, you continue asking questions related to their specific needs.

If you don't have a business card, postcard, or flyer, then use your phone to share an electronic business card, your website, and social media.

Example #1.1 Approaching people with your cellphone (exchange phone number, website, and/ or social media)

You—Hello, how are you?

Them—Good.

You—Nice to meet you, my name is_____.

Them—Nice to meet you.

You—I am a real estate professional in this area. Are you or do you know anyone who is interested in buying, selling, or renting any property right now?

Them—Yes or no (wait and listen)

* If the answer is **NO:**

Good, thank you very much for listening to me. I would like to send my information through text of my (website, social media page, etc.) for you to keep my information in case in the future you might need my services or know someone who does.

*If **YES:**

I would like to have your phone number so we can communicate better. We can make an appointment, or I could send you a free list of available properties. Your number is? ....
(Wait till they give it to you).

Once they give you the phone number, if there's time and they can, ask them some questions like:

What are you looking for?

What do you need?

The main purpose is to get their phone number so you can follow up with them later. Since these people are working, you may forget to ask for their phone number if you do not ask for it first.

Example #2:

- You are waiting to be taken care of, either in a doctor's office, at the dentist, accountant, lawyer, or in line at the supermarket. This time, the person you are approaching is the person in front of you, behind you, or waiting with you in a waiting room.
- Choose who you will address, since every person who is one meter (three feet) from you will be a possible prospect.

Step to approach while standing in line or waiting for an appointment:

1. Make eye contact before talking to the prospect. (If they see you, speak to them. Otherwise, wait for them to give eye contact before you speak to them.)
2. After you establish eye contact, do a semi smile. (You do this to see if the person is nice. If they don't smile back, they may be an unpleasant person and someone you'd rather not know.)
3. Finally, speak to the prospect after they smile back at you.

These steps happen quickly. Soon you will do them out of inertia and habit without realizing it, but at first, realize your goal is to work with nice people. You are the one who chooses your customers, and you might as well work with nice ones.

In a Department Store

Start a conversation with a person while you are in line at the store:

You—Hello! What a long line. (This example works if the line is long. You can also comment about the weather, the specials of the day, or the dress or shirt the person is wearing. You could ask where they bought it. Let the conversation flow, and always remember to immediately give them your business card, or exchange your information by phone, email, or social media.)

Them—Yeah, that's true.

You—I want to give you my business card (or information through your electronic device). I am a real estate professional. Maybe you know of someone who needs my services?

Them—Thank you.

You—Are you a homeowner?

Them—Yes or No

Whatever the answer, the most important thing is to start the conversation, so you can get their phone number. Your goal is to create a database. They may not be interested today, but they could be interested at another time or know someone who is interested now. They may be a valuable resource for referrals.

*If the answer is **yes**, I am a homeowner:

You—That's great! Since when? (Keep asking questions until you know if they might be interested in buying another home or selling the one they currently own. They may know of a neighbor who wants to sell their home.)

*If the answer is **No**:

You—Well, would you like to buy a house?

The conversation continues:

You—What might work best is for you to give me your phone number so I can send you a list of properties for sale or rent that might fill your criteria. (Customize what you send them, depending on their needs.)

- Have your phone readily available every time you approach people so you're ready to send your information to their phone.
- Continue to socialize with other professional people you know such as **doctors, dentists, teachers (even your children's), other parents, church members, club members, people at the gym, people at sports events, instructors, friends, referrals, and family members.**

Example 3:

Your circle of influence, professionals, and family

Doctors' office:

Doctor—How are you?

You—Good. How about you?

Doctor—Good...

You—(In a routine checkup) I want to give you my business card (or your information, the way you want to approach them, such as your cell phone number, etc.) in case you know of someone who is interested in my services. I am a real estate professional with extensive experience in (whatever you want to specialize in or say if you want to specify your expertise.)

Doctor—Good, how is the market?

You—Excellent. Are you interested in buying or selling, doctor?

—If the doctor says they're interested in buying or selling, continue the conversation until you get their phone number and an appointment.

—If the doctor says they're not interested in buying or selling, tell them you would love to receive any referrals if they know someone.

Also ask if they would allow you to put your business cards in their waiting room.

*This script can be used for all types of professionals who provide services like attorneys, doctors, accountants, and more. You can adjust the script to your own needs and personal style.

Calling Your Friends, Family, and Other Contacts

Of course, you will be speaking with friends and family in person, but it's also important to call them with different variations of information and questions. If they are not interested, ask them for references and add them to your database including their phone number, business and home address, and email.

It's also helpful to send them additional information, either by mail or email. Many boards, clubs, and professional associations of realtors offer informative newsletters; make sure to mention you'll be sending them useful updates about the real estate market, and that's why you'd like to keep their contact information on file.

- Before calling, make sure your energy level and mood are up. When you are cheerful, you will attract more appointments and have better results. (People like to talk with cheerful people.)
- Believe it or not, even if the other person is not looking at you when you call them on the phone, it is not the same to call them while you're standing up as it is while you're lying down. When someone calls you and you are lying down, they will ask you if you were asleep or are sick or tired, even when you are not.
- The clothes you are wearing should not squeeze your stomach. Physical discomfort could be reflected in your energy level or be bothersome for you. If your clothes tighten your waist, unbutton the button.

There are three ways to raise your energy before you place the call:

1. Hop or jog around a bit before calling (this will help you lift your energy level).
2. View your earlier results and say them aloud. Example: I am grateful for setting up three appointments today!
3. Thank God beforehand for the appointments and people He will put in your path today for your success.

*Some people have a special playlist or song they listen to before calling. This lifts their spirits and puts them on top of the world. Whatever you do, make sure it works for you. At first, you will need to prepare your mindset before making calls. The first step is always **action**; after 30 days, this action becomes a **discipline**; after three months, it will be a **habit**; after six months, you will no longer be able to live without calling, and it will be part of you, your **passion. "ADHP" (ACTION, DISCIPLINE, HABIT, PASSION).**

Example 1, Your close circle: calling friends, family members, etc.

If you're new to the real estate business:

You—Hello_____, this is _____. How are you? The reason for my call is to let you know I just started in the real estate business. I was wondering if you or someone you know might need my services. (Wait for their response.)

Them—If **Yes.**

You—Fabulous! Which day is better to talk in more detail so I can give you the time you deserve? **Do you prefer Thursday or Saturday?** (Do not talk, just listen.)

You—Perfect, I will see you on Saturday. Do you prefer the morning or afternoon? (Expect him/her to respond.)

You—Excellent! I will see you Saturday at 3:00 p.m.

Let me confirm your address_____.

You—Thank you very much! See you soon.

If they tell you **No**, then you say:

You—Perfect, but would it be ok if I mailed you (or emailed you) information about my services? I just need to verify your email and mailing address.

After you have their data, put it in your database and create an advertising campaign. Let them know you also emailed your information so they will not be surprised.

- Try to keep the conversation short. Because you are working, you will want to schedule as many appointments as possible in the shortest possible time. If you keep talking, they could cancel the appointment.
- You could use a sandglass at first, to remind you to keep your conversation short. Explain the reason for your call, make the appointment, get referrals, and update your data so you can send them more information by regular mail or email. You can also share your phone number, website, social media pages, and any other related information you have.

- Giving two options for the appointment day and time will make it easier for them to book the appointment. While you're on the call, control the conversation. It's best to offer times to your contact instead of accepting a time that works for them but not for you. **Every time you make an appointment, always remember to give options (example: today or tomorrow).** If instead you ask, "When do you want to meet?" the person will start thinking about everything they have to do. You'll be lucky if they give you the appointment in a couple of *months*.

- When you give options, the brain focuses only on the options; that is why you get the appointment. If for some reason, the person evades setting up the appointment, ask another question in the same way, giving options: "What do you prefer, weekdays or weekends?"

Example #2 Calling

If you've been in the real estate business for a while:

You—Hi_____, do you have a minute? Guess what? I've told you I am a real estate professional, right?
I am excited because I have a big goal in my business this month to work with 10 new clients to help them in any area, whether it's buying, selling, or renting, and I would love if you could help me with my goal.

I do not know if you or someone you know is interested in any of the areas I mentioned to you. There is no obligation for them to work with me, of course, but do you know someone who might possibly need my service? Maybe it's your neighbor, friend, or family member. (Wait till they respond. Do not talk while they are thinking. If you talk, you lose.)

As soon as they mention someone to you, immediately ask for the contact information of that person, and thank them for their help.

Additional step

You—Thank you so much for your help. I was hoping I could count on you to help me reach my goal.

—I would like to send you some information by text, regular mail, or email. What is your email address? (Wait for answer.)

You—_____, perfect. Your address is_____. Goodbye and thank you again, _____. (If you have their address, you'll be able to run a comparable in case they want to sell their property.)

- If they are the ones who are interested in selling or buying, use the two-option method from before.

You—Would you like to meet in my office or at your house? (Expect them to respond. Remember not to talk.)

You—Perfect. Monday or Tuesday?

*And so on.

Good luck!

Scheduling coffee and lunch appointments can be great ways to maximize your time and discuss your client's real estate needs.

In addition, there are two convenient hours to call potential clients: one at 9:00 a.m. and another in the afternoon at 4:00 p.m. Use the 9 a.m. time to call clients from the coffee shop.

Why make calls in a public place? For three simple reasons:

1. You start your work in public early, with your professional team ready and willing to help you. If someone calls you or you're on a call and they want to meet right now, you will waste no time getting dressed.

Why not call from the office while drinking your coffee?

The coffee shop will give you an additional option the office does not give you:

2. You have the option of approaching people to give them your electronic information or business card, plus any advertising you have on hand. This is instrumental to the success of your business. Remember the saying, "Don't put all your eggs in one basket."

The afternoon is a good time to call from the office or your home.

What is the third reason?

3. When you meet people in the coffee shop while you are calling new clients, it will help you expand your business. At the coffee shop, you can handle new clients after your calls, during, or before your calls, depending on how it suits you. It's like double-booking your calls while you're meeting influential people, "Killing two birds with one stone."

Let the person know you have another appointment after them in Zoom or Google Meet. (If you say another person is coming but they don't show up, the person will see that no one came. If instead you say the next meeting is via Zoom and the other person doesn't show up, your current contact will never know.) Your time is limited, and you must make the most of your time, even if the person scheduled after them doesn't show. Manage your time intelligently and effectively. This is essential to your success.

The appointments you make can be in Zoom, Google Meet, or any other meeting type you like. These meetings allow you to help buyers and tenants prequalify and find properties on the MLS. You'll be able to show them prices and property locations in real time. You can also immediately save all the searches, create an email automatically, and make the appointment through a showing assistant if it is available. Try not to use online meetings for sellers or landlords who are in your area because you will need to inspect the properties and get the listings when you are doing the listing presentations. Online meetings are a great option when sellers or landlords live far from you or in another county, state, or country.

Make lunch appointments at least two to three times a week with someone influential to your business. They may offer help with referrals, or perhaps they are friends who know people who can help you grow your business.

Remember: Your work is urgent and important. Put your social relationships to work in your favor and learn how to profit from your network.

Chapter 4

Plan for Success

If you want to be successful, avoid these mistakes:

- Don't allow your goal or mission to be one just one more thing you haven't achieved.
- The mission must be yours and not anyone else's. It won't work if this is your family's, spouse's, or society's goal for you.
- Don't forget about it or set it aside.
- Avoid using phrases like, "I must…" Use more encouraging words like, "I like to do...," "I enjoy..." "I am glad to have a lot of work..."

Vision Board/Action Board Examples:

What Is a Vision Board?

A vision board is a tool that will give you a clearer view of what you want to attract in your business and your life. It shows where you want to be and accelerates and focuses the process, so the miracle is performed.

It is the secret weapon to achieve your goals. You can do everything you set out to do, even if your dreams are big. Just know anything is possible if you believe it. If it is in your mind, you can do it. *There is nothing you cannot do if your mind can see it.*

If you lack action and a plan, your dreams won't be realized. When you focus on your plan and work on it, your goal will be an imminent reality.

Before You Start Your Vision Board

Before you start, imagine you are not afraid and that anything is possible. Now write down what you want to achieve for this year and visualize it.

Write the areas you want to improve:

Example: God, yourself, your family, career/business, love, travel, the house you want, the car, etc.

- Look for magazines, applications, and online clippings of all the places that you like and want, such as your home, places to travel, money, etc.
- Search for photos of yourself and, if you want, your family, and photos of houses, cars, and places you like.
- For my vision board, I like to personalize it by including pictures of myself. I like to add my name to it and make it personal because it is mine.

Example:

In the **Me** section, I add my photo with the body I want to have, instead of using the photo of the model with her face. I completely cut off the face of the model; now I am the model.

I do the same with the car. I find a car I like, then place my photo next to the car. Then I take a photo of the car and me together and print a new photo. It looks like it is already my car. I'm either driving it or standing next to it. This is how I trick my subconscious mind. I travel into the future by making it an immediate and imminent present.

In the **family** section, I like to crop some photos showing my family united and happy.

Some people visualize about **love.** They draw what is an ideal couple for them. Put your own creation here.

I like to play with my **age**. I cut photos of myself 10–20 years younger to imagine that I am getting younger and younger, as if time has stopped.

The best idea is for you to create your vision board in the way you feel best.

- Look for apps for your computer or phone that will easily put all your photos together if you do not want to create them manually. Use online tools like Canva.com to create your vision board.
- Look for positive phrases on the internet that motivate you and print them or write them down with your own handwriting to give an extra boost to your goal setting.
- Write yourself a check for the amount you want to earn and paste it on your board.
- Buy a large or medium board so you can put everything you want on it.
- Have supplies handy: scissors, glue, tape, your photos, clippings, pencils, markers, etc.
- Be precise and detailed about what you want.
- Sketch your vision board layout before you start it on paper or place it without pasting it so you can visualize and move the images wherever you want.

Believe in what you're going to attract into your life. Put what you think is possible, without limiting yourself. You know yourself better than anyone.

Remember to add affirmations to your real estate business such as:

- I am a multimillion-dollar producer.
- I am a top producer.
- I am the best seller in my office, city, year, (whatever you want).
- Add everything you think will help you achieve your goals.
- Find something you accomplished in your past and add it to your vision board to remind you that you can do it now with real estate and do it even better.

When your board is finished, hang it up somewhere so you'll see it often. For example: if you put it in your bedroom, you will see it when you go to sleep and when you wake up. Also, take a photo of it with your cellphone so you can see it every time you open your phone or visit your gallery.

If you do not want to do your vision board with paper and glue, find programs and apps to make it electronically.

Go to the Play Store and type "vision," "the law of attraction," "my vision board," and more. The most important thing is to do it and have it visible. You could even print it and have a framed copy.

The vision board has been used by many successful people who were initially skeptical and did not want to use it, but they decided they wouldn't lose anything if they would just try it. When they did, their businesses and lives changed in powerful ways. Here are some examples:

Jim Carrey—In the 1990s, Jim Carrey was an unknown actor with no money. In a later interview with Oprah Winfrey, he explained his visualization process, "I wrote myself a check for $10 million for 'acting services rendered' and I gave myself 5 years ... or 3 years maybe. I dated it Thanksgiving 1995 and I put it in my wallet and I kept it there and it deteriorated and deteriorated. But then, just before Thanksgiving 1995, I found out that I was going to make $10 million on *Dumb and Dumber*."[1] Carrey says his success was due to visualization, leading him to become one of the highest-paid stars in Hollywood.

Arnold Schwarzenegger—Arnold used this visualization method several times in his life to get what he wanted. The first time was when he was a young athlete. He wanted to be like Reg Park. The more he focused on this image and worked out, the more he grew. The more he saw the picture, the more real it became to be like Reg Park. Thanks to this visualization, he became a champion in bodybuilding. He used it twice more, once when he became an actor and the other when he entered politics. He says he uses visualization for everything.

Oprah Winfrey—This media magnate, who grew up in poverty, became one of the richest women in the world. She could be one of the greatest supporters of **affirmation.** Her commitment to affirmations started from a young age. When she was a child, she saw her grandmother worn out and

---

1 https://www.cheatsheet.com/entertainment/why-jim-carrey-wrote-himself-a-10-million-check-before-he-was-famous.html/

in poverty. Winfrey said to herself repeatedly, "My life won't be like this. My life won't be like this, it **will be better.**"[2]

In addition, she frequently highlighted the power of positive thought through success stories on her program. She even discussed how to create your own vision board to realize your dreams. Her many words of wisdom to her fans include, **"Create the highest, grandest vision possible for your life because you become what you believe."**[3]

Lindsey Vonn—One of the most successful female skiers in history, the gold medal winner says her mental practice gives her a competitive edge in the course. Vonn says, "I always visualize the run before I do it. By the time I get to the start gate, I've run that race 100 times already in my head, picturing how I'll take the turns."[4]

She does not just keep the images in her head; she also does physical simulation by literally shifting her weight back and forth as if she were on the skis. She also practices the breathing patterns she uses during the race. "I love that exercise," says Vonn. "Once I visualize a course, I never forget it. So I get on those lines and go through exactly the run that I want to have. I control my emotions and just make it routine."[5]

Will Smith—A great advocate of the law of attraction, the award-winning actor says his positive thoughts have helped him achieve happiness. "In my mind, I've always been an A-list Hollywood superstar. Y'all just didn't know yet."[6] Smith says visualization techniques have helped him throughout his life.

He also cites Confucius' motivating motto to explain his success at the box office: "The man who says he can, and the man who says he can't are both correct."

As you will notice, having a vision board, using encouraging words, acting as if it is already yours, and being positive, will all lead you to success. *If they can do it, so can you!*

---

2 https://enjoymutable.com/home/elonmuskchinaandthemultiverse

3 https://quoteinvestigator.com/2019/08/25/grandest/

4 https://www.forbes.com/sites/vanessaloder/2014/07/23/the-power-of-vision-what-entrepreneurs-can-learn-from-olympic-athletes/?sh=645a92ad6e74

5 https://www.si.com/more-sports/2010/02/17/vonn

6 https://www.goalcast.com/20-will-smith-quotes-that-will-inspire-you/

Vision Board Framework

Use this framework to guide you if you have never done a vision board or if you have made one but were not happy with the one you had.

The first thing to do is to define your priorities. These may be current priorities or future habits you want to cultivate.

The vision board can be done in different ways depending on how your brain works or how you feel most comfortable. You can divide the board into imaginary sections according to your priorities or create a board without dividers if you want this vision board to just focus on your career. Some people like to have all their goals divided into several sections (six, four, two, or just one section to focus on one thing at a time). At the end of the book, I include a resource section with four different ways to organize your vision board.

Example:

Personally, I have two boards, but as an example I will share the one I organized into six sections. Each section consists of images, photos, and words that lead me to what I want to improve and achieve (customize yours according to your goals and beliefs):

1. God, 2. Myself, 3. Family, 4. Career/Abundance, 5. Charity, 6. Fun.

You can place your partner, love, and romance in whichever category you want, depending on which value they fulfill, but always put God first, and yourself second. Love may be in the section with yourself if you are married or in a stable relationship. If you are single and do not have a partner, it may be in the family section or in fun, depending on where you want it.

God#1 Priority

- Images that represent your communication and connection with God.

Example: Your church, the Holy Spirit, whatever you feel expresses your goals the best in words or drawings.

Priority #2 ME

Include photographs of yourself to give your vision board a personal touch and credibility to what you personally want. When I create mine, I cut my face out and place it on the body I want to look like to either lose weight or tone my muscles. Work on:

- Self-love, self-esteem, self-respect, and giving respect
- Image you want to project
- Health
- The perfect love
- Drawings, letters, and images...

Family #3 Priority

- Include what you want. Do you want to keep the family as it is currently or to cultivate better relationships?
- Add photos of joyful moments.
- If you do not have a family yet, how would you wish it to be?

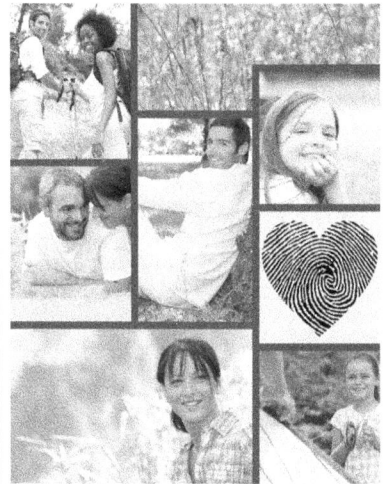

Priority #4 Wealth/Career/Degree

Include words that signify greatness, success, wealth, and abundance.

- Photos of the house, investments, car, money, and career you want.
- Events, actions, and projects that you want to realize.
- Studies, designations, degrees.
- Be specific with your photos. What will the house look like inside? Include a check with the amount you desire to have.
- Logos/photos/recognition images like #1 Realtor, Best Salesperson, etc.

Charity #5 Priority

- Institutions, organizations and/or places where you wish to contribute.
- Where you want to donate your time to the community.
- Include photos, images, logos, etc.

Priority #6 Fun (Positive Pleasures)

- Include travel, places you want to go, friendships, etc.
- Imagine what you like to do.
- Hobbies, sports, love/romance.
- This is a way to reward yourself for all your hard work.

Visualization Exercise

Find a comfortable place (this could be your house, the beach, or any restful spot such as your bed or a recliner). Put on comfortable clothes and cover up with a sheet if you are cold.

Breathe through your nose and exhale through your mouth at least three to five times. When you exhale, say to yourself, "I am more and more deeply relaxed."

Now visualize a place that is pleasant and gives you peace. When you find that image and feel it, visualize the kind of life you want to have both in your personal life and in your business. Today I want you to see the type of agent you want to be as if you already are this successful agent, an agent who sells millions of dollars in property.

Imagine you live in the house you want, thanks to God and your work. Imagine the kind of car you drive to your appointments. Imagine how your car smells, its color, and how well it drives.

Think of the clothes you are wearing as you show the properties you would like to show, in the neighborhood you would like to work, and signing sales contracts with customers in the areas where you specialize from now on.

You are now at the property closing and are collecting the closing check. You receive your commission check each week in an envelope. When you open the envelope, you're happy to see several checks in there, as you have multiple sales transactions. Now imagine some of your commissions are wire transferred. Visualize yourself logging into your bank account and you can see all the commissions deposited in green. Your bank account has more money now.

Imagine your family. See the smiles on their faces as you gather to enjoy each other's company. Feel the love in the room and the warmth of your love towards them.

Continue like this until you feel joy inside you. Go as far as you want or until you feel it and believe it is your new reality.

At the end, breathe three times and affirm the following out loud:

"I am happy; I am blessed; I am successful."

Open your eyes with positive energy. You are now ready for success.

Goals, Objectives, and Your Mission: Short, Medium, and Long-term

Long-term goals: This is your life project. You can divide the goal(s) over a period of one, three, five, or ten years.

You must consider all timeframes in your planning (long, medium, and short), but for now we'll concentrate on annual goals.

Ask yourself these questions:

1. What do I want to do in my real estate business?

_____

_____

_____

2. Who do I want to be? Who do I want to become?

_____

_____

_____

3. What results do I want to see in my business?

_____

_____

_____

4. What do I want in my personal life?

_____

_____

_____

5. What do I want to have materially? Example: house, car, awards, success in your business, etc.

_____

_____

_____

6. How far do I want to go in my career?

_____

_____

_____

This is a good way to affirm your goals:

This year, 20__, from January 1 to December 31, I want to earn **$100,000.00.** (This is the amount you think you can make based on the time you will work in your real estate business. Make it big enough to stretch you, but at the same time, it should be believable for you and coordinated with the time you can devote to your business.)

Divide the amount into timeframes and create your own plan based on the time you have.

Let us say you have 20 hours a week to devote to your real estate business. Two of the days you should work are Saturday and Sunday, because they're the best for open houses, appointments, and showing homes. You will want to devote at least two more days during the week to real estate. Make calls on those days. Call, call, call, until you get five appointments for the weekend and five for your working weekdays. Use a specialized real estate planner, so you can record your calls and meet your goals.

Stick to your goal. It's the only way to achieve what you want.

Within your long-term goal, you include goals for studying, working on a degree, training, obtaining awards, and participating in clubs to expand your clientele.

Include the number of people you will approach when you are eating, at the store, etc. Remember to talk with at least five people per day to share information about your business. Realtors are working all the time, even when they are out with friends and family. When you leave home is when you will be handing out cards and talking with people. You never know when the person in front of you will become a customer who is worth thousands of dollars in income, either because of their business or their referrals.

Example of How to Set Up Your Planner

Saturday

8:00 a.m.–8:55 a.m. Search a list of properties for customers and/or Comparables/CMA (Comparable Market Analysis for sellers)

9:00 a.m.–10:00 a.m. Appointments

10:30 a.m.–1:00 p.m. Property showings/ Listing presentations/Open houses

1:00 p.m.–2:00 p.m. Lunch/free time

2:00 p.m.–5:00 p.m. Property showings/Listing presentations/Open houses

5:00 p.m.–6:00 p.m. Free time/computer search

6:00 p.m.–7:30 p.m. Optional, if you want to see another customer

Use all the free time you have on Saturday to keep prospecting, calling, and talking to people at the places you visit.

Sunday

Many people go to church on Sunday. Coordinate with your clients in advance to know the best schedule for them. Check the mass or service schedule with the church. Make sure to respect your client's church time and go to church yourself if it's part of your spiritual practice.

You can repeat the same schedule as Saturday. See three clients, visit an open house, or see fewer customers. If you want to dedicate yourself to real estate full time or have a large financial goal, you will want to see clients on Sunday. Be sure to dedicate yourself to your goal if you want to see it achieved.

Weekday Example: Mondays and Wednesdays (If You're Working Part-Time on Your Real Estate Business)

Monday

6:00 a.m.–7:00 a.m. Work on your real estate business by searching properties, emailing new clients, doing CMAs, etc.

7:00 a.m–8:00 a.m. Get ready for your corporate job

8:00 a.m.–9:00 a.m. While driving, listen to something motivational such as affirmations or positive books, etc.

9:00 a.m.–12:00 p.m. Corporate work

12:01 p.m.–1:00 p.m. Lunch. Contact customers, send emails, make calls, prepare presentations, etc. (Do these activities if you have time, depending on the work you do.)

1:00 p.m.–5:00 p.m. Corporate work

5:00 p.m.–8:00 p.m. Drive, work on any real estate activities, make calls to clients for at least 1-2 hours, see clients, etc. If you visit a client, you might not have time to call or split the time block if the appointment with your client is quick.

9:00 p.m.–10:00 p.m. Social media marketing in general (carousel posts, reels, pictures, videos, etc.), private messaging, posting. Do this at least 3-6 days a week.

Wednesday

Repeat the same schedule as Monday unless something changes, and you need to be more flexible. Try to follow the same work pattern and stick to your schedule. Imagine you are already being paid $100,000.00 if you're working full-time in real estate or $50,000.00 working part-time.

*Biweekly, write yourself a check for the work you do by dividing $100,000.00 ($3,846.15) or $50,000.00 ($1,923.07) into 26 weeks. If you prefer payment twice per month, write yourself a check on the first and the fifteenth: this is 24 checks per year at $100,000.00 ($4,166.66) or $50,000.00 ($2,083.33). Collect all the checks for 90 days and start paying yourself after 90 days if you did all your work and worked for either 40 hours per week full-time or 20 hours per week part-time. If you failed (you didn't do the work and weren't committed to your goal), you will have to start the 90-day process all over again. Continue collecting your checks either every fifteen days or biweekly and pay yourself.

You will see that within 90 days of doing this, you will be able to collect your first check, and it will continue this way for the rest of your career.

How to Write Your Check

Write your first biweekly (or two checks a month) after you have worked, as you would in any job for which you are paid. In all jobs, the first check is stored as a deposit, so the first check you receive will be in 30 days. Write the deposit check and keep it as a deposit in case you need it in the future.

Then, after 90 days and you have met your goal, start collecting the first check and continue this biweekly until you are earning the same or more.

If for some reason you think you cannot achieve your desired money goal, do not worry; try to do it for the first 90 days. If your schedule does not allow you to devote enough time to your business, lower the amount of money you want to make.

Remember, the most important thing is not that you've earned the first $100,000.00 or $50,000.00 in real estate; instead, the most important thing is to develop the habit of believing in yourself and your ability to achieve your goals. When you reach your goal this year at the desired amount, you can continue to apply the same method and start increasing the amount, according to your time commitment and business goals.

Medium-term goals: Goals that are achieved within 3-6 months. You can develop and work on these goals with a clear vision. For example, divide your quarterly results into a specific amount of revenue, sales, or closings.

Short-term goals: Expected short-term achievements that can happen within a month or two. For example, the goal might be to make five appointments in a month, write two contracts this month, or have your first closing in the next 90 days. Obviously, this short-term goal will support a long-term goal that can be achieved because you first achieved the short-term goal.

Objective: Being clear about your business goals is so important because it will keep you from wasting time on unnecessary activities. For example: if your goal is to specialize in exclusively representing sellers, you should not be working in the renter market. Knowing and being clear about your goals will help you get more sellers as clients. Keep a list of realtors who specialize in working with buyers, and a list of realtors who work with tenants. Send those lists to your prospect instead of trying to help everyone.

For the realtors you refer, sign a referral agreement at either 25% or more, depending on whether you only give them the customer or do something else. That way, you will have more time to dedicate yourself to your goal and be able to specialize in your target market, while still receiving money for the referrals.

In the end, you will earn more money because you will have multiple income sources. Plus, you will look more professional to your clients. At first, if you try to do it all, you will have a difficult time letting go of customers, but you must be clear about your goal (or change your goal).

Mission: Your mission is your legacy, a life's mission both personally and professionally. They must be connected and related to succeed. If your personal and professional missions do not connect, you will experience obstacles in one or both areas. If you have a life partner, be sure to tell them about your mission. If your partner is not willing to help you achieve your mission, the least they can do is not actively harm your goal. Explain how important it is for you to achieve your mission. Let them know, so you're both on the same page.

Direction/Vision: Having a clear vision about your business is like having a map or GPS that already knows the way to the finish line. You cannot detour or avoid the road to reach your destination. You must identify the path to be charted so you know when you're off track. You'll want to re-evaluate each month or quarter to keep going in the right direction.

Time You Need vs. Time You Have

To be effective, you must know how to manage time intelligently by learning how to prioritize. Evaluate your work activities not as they arise, but by their importance to your work and business.

When you start in this business or do not have enough customers, use the 80/20 rule. Use 80% of your time to prospect and 20% of your time for the rest of your activities as a real estate agent, such as showings, searching for properties, and running reports.

Example:

For the upcoming month, mark non-negotiable activities in your planner. Non-negotiable activities have high-level results, such as generating new clients or opportunities. Remember to prioritize action, discipline, habit, and passion.

Ideal Daily Schedule

8:00 a.m.–9:00 a.m. Social media postings, private messages, interactions about your business at least five days a week

9:00 a.m.–10:00 a.m. Make calls Monday and Wednesday

4:00 p.m.–5:00 p.m. Make calls on Tuesday and Thursday (Start any time from 4:00 p.m. to 8:30 p.m. Modify your call start time according to your appointments and make appointments in between in-person meetings.)

9:00 p.m.–10:00 p.m. Post on social media, use videos, carousel posts, etc. Use this time block if you were busy during the day and couldn't post earlier.

Schedule the rest of your activities according to your other obligations but treat calls and marketing as priority items because they will result in new clients. Be sure to block out time on your calendar for marketing so you treat it like any other important appointment.

Action Plan (A Plan Tailored to You)

Having an action plan will help you prioritize the most important activities to meet your objectives and goals. This guide will provide a framework for how to carry out your projects and get the desired results.

In your plan, include who is responsible for each activity. If it's just you, put your name there. If you have a partner or assistant, designate who will do each activity by recording their name next to it.

Any action plan should include the strategies, projects, actions, resources, start date and end date, and who executes the job. You can adjust it to your business and create your own action plan but be sure to include the information listed above.

Examples:

Operational Plan			
What to do? Objectives	**How to do it?** Activities	**When to do it?** Dates	**With what resources?**
Hire a partner/agent to work as a team and divide clients by specialization.	Recruit, interview, select the right agent. Find someone compatible in the business.	July 1-30	Ad in the office, database, real estate agent magazines, LinkedIn, social media.
Hire an assistant for both.	Interviews, select the most competent with a minimum of one year of experience.	August 1-30	Zip Recruiter, newspaper, LinkedIn, social media/networks, and the internet.

Action Plan Activities						
Specific objective	**Activity**	**Strategies**	**Resources**	**Responsible**	**Date**	**Evaluation**
Close 30 agreements in a year	Buyers Sellers	Working with a team or at least one partner	Redx Bresser calls, mail, social media, YouTube	partner and me	July 1, 2022 to June 31, 2023	Split the work. Example: partner works with buyers, and I work with sellers

Adapt your operational and action plans to your needs. Add more columns if you need it to be more specific to your plan. Use it to guide your actions and follow it to achieve your goals.

Agenda

Get a planner that you like to manage your contacts with your customers. If you do not like a paper calendar, pick an electronic calendar alternative for your cell phone, computer, or iPad, such as Google Calendar. A bonus three-month specialized agenda for realtors and brokers is included at the end of this book. If you like it, consider purchasing my Agent's Success Planner, 52-Week Undated Agenda.

Plan your work one month ahead. Try using a pen to mark the things you will not change, such as morning calls, and use a pencil to mark appointments and afternoon calls that may change according to client needs.

Your agenda must have a space to record the most important activities that need to be done each day. Three to five small lines will suffice. As the day goes by, you can cross them out as you create your most productive, useful, and organized day. Write them from most important to least important (and try to complete the most important ones first).

Managing your time in an organized and consistent way, ahead of time, is essential if you want productive results in your business.

When you pick a planner, it needs to have at minimum:

- You must like it and identify with the theme.
- One column per day, if you write a lot.
- A space to list the most important activities to complete that day.
- Enough space to write appointments by the hour if you work full time.
- Write your own affirmations each month and repeat them each day for 30 days.
- Add all the goals you want to accomplish each month. At the end of the month, compare the goals you set at the beginning of the month to your results.
- Record the calls/contacts/clients goal log to compare your results from month to month. Write what you learned each month to track your progress, so by the end of the year you will see how much you advanced and know what areas to improve, and which areas need your attention. Finally, write your monthly results.

- Write your affirmation of the week and repeat it every day for seven days. The weekly affirmation must coordinate with the monthly affirmation if you want it to work. You can have several affirmations and rotate them each week or month.
- In the priorities section, record the most important activities to perform that day, whether they are activities that produce income or personal satisfaction.
- The last part at the bottom of the page is to record and evaluate your week to keep you focused on your daily business activities.

You can have an electronic agenda, but I recommend having one that you can write in, even if you use it just the first year, to create a new habit.

Approaches/Posts/Calls Goal Tracking

Start	1	2	3	4	5
	6	7	8	9	10
	11	12	13	14	15
	16	17	18	19	20
	21	22	23	24	25
	26	27	28	29	30
	31	32	33	34	35
	36	37	38	39	40
	41	42	43	44	45
Goal	46	47	48	49	50

Monthly Realized Goals

- [ ] ______
- [ ] ______
- [ ] ______
- [ ] ______
- [ ] ______
- [ ] ______
- [ ] ______
- [ ] ______
- [ ] ______

What did you learn this month?

______

______

______

______

______

______

______

______

______

Results:

______

______

______

Month: _____

Monday	Tuesday	Wednesday	Thursday	Friday
☐	☐	☐	☐	☐
☐	☐	☐	☐	☐
☐	☐	☐	☐	☐
☐	☐	☐	☐	☐
☐	☐	☐	☐	☐

Number of Monthly Goals Reached:

_____ Social Media Posts   _____ Handed Out Business Cards   _____ New Contracts

_____ Calls   _____ Appointments   _____ Purchases

_____ Talked to People   _____ Listing Presentations   _____ Rentals

_____ New Contacts   _____ Listings   _____ Referrals

20_____

Monthly Goals

Saturday	Sunday
☐	☐
☐	☐
☐	☐
☐	☐
☐	☐

☐ _____
☐ _____
☐ _____
☐ _____
☐ _____
☐ _____

Monthly To-Do List

☐ _____
☐ _____
☐ _____
☐ _____
☐ _____
☐ _____
☐ _____
☐ _____
☐ _____
☐ _____

NOTES:

Monthly Affirmation: _____

Week of:_____

Priorities	Monday _____	Tuesday _____	Wednesday _____	Thursday _____
	☐	☐	☐	☐
	☐	☐	☐	☐
	☐	☐	☐	☐
	☐	☐	☐	☐
	☐	☐	☐	☐
	☐	☐	☐	☐
8				
9				
10				
11				
12				
1				
2				
3				
4				
5				
6				
7				

Number of Weekly Goals Reached:

_____Social Media Posts	_____Handed Out Business Cards	_____New Contracts
_____Calls	_____Appointments	_____Purchases
_____Talked to People	_____Listing Presentations	_____Rentals
_____New Contacts	_____Listings	_____Referrals

Month: _____

Friday _____	Saturday _____	Sunday _____
☐	☐	☐
☐	☐	☐
☐	☐	☐
☐	☐	☐
☐	☐	☐
☐	☐	☐
8		
9		
10		
11		
12		
1		
2		
3		
4		
5		
6		
7		

Weekly Goals

☐ _____
☐ _____
☐ _____
☐ _____
☐ _____
☐ _____
☐ _____
☐ _____

Weekly To-Do List

☐ _____
☐ _____
☐ _____
☐ _____
☐ _____
☐ _____
☐ _____
☐ _____
☐ _____
☐ _____

NOTES:

_____
_____
_____
_____
_____
_____

Weekly Affirmation: _____

_____
_____
_____
_____
_____

The Big Day: "Opening Your Business"

For those who are starting, restarting, or have never had a business debut.

One mistake some real estate agents make is not to treat their business like a business. If you look at any establishment, they start announcing the grand opening of their business before they open. When the opening day comes, they already have people ready to attend. Treat your business like a big business, do a grand opening, and reap the financial benefits.

Opening Ceremony

Your grand opening will give you the right start and generate customers from that day or even before, when you start inviting people to attend. Invite everyone you know: neighbors, family, friends, and friends of your friends. They will become your first customers. In addition, hand out referral sheets to each guest as they arrive. Tell them each referral they share will give them an entry ticket in a raffle. The more they refer, the more chances they have to win a prize. Buy your own gifts or talk to companies that might donate prizes. Tell these companies you will recommend them and mention them in your grand opening. Examples of companies that might donate include: your broker, title companies, attorneys, schools of real estate, construction companies, insurance agents, and more.

When you send the invitation, tell your guests that you would love it if they would bring a guest(s) with them. Their guests could be their family, friends, and / or people they know who are looking for real estate services.

The grand opening is an initial kickoff of luck, celebration, and networking. Your new business starts with your professional and personal touch. It is your time to shine.

Suggestions

- Celebrate your achievements and ask someone else to read your bio for you. This person could be your broker or office manager, or someone you consider influential in your life.
- Prepare an influential and brief speech. Focus on your clients' benefits by highlighting the activities you did to help them succeed. Start by thanking them and letting them know how important clients are in your personal and professional life.

- Your story should illustrate who you are and what motivated you to start your real estate business. Consider your passion and long-term real estate goals.

- Talk about your company and your broker. Share the support they give you and how it benefits you and your clients. Show how you are supported throughout this journey one hundred percent.

- If you decided to have a team, mention who they are and what they do.

- Keep your business opening as simple as possible.

- If you want, before the clients begin arriving, have a PowerPoint presentation playing that shows the services you offer, the properties you have for sale, or show a general slide with an introduction to real estate.

- Always dress professionally when you work with clients.

- Keep costs as low as possible. Your grand opening is not the time to throw the house out the window; its goal is to make you known among your acquaintances and common interest holders that you are active in your business, are professional, and have all the tools you need for success. Use this opportunity to set the tone from now on with your customers.

- Have a few snacks, appetizers, refreshments, and something to drink for a toast.

- On the invitation, mention this will be a two-hour event, so they should arrive on time as the event is only for two hours.

- Use the suggested agenda in the book or make your own and be precise with your event timing. Send this agenda to your guests so they know how the event will proceed and know to come on time. They should be prepared for their own pre-qualification, property search, and to ask questions.

- In the invitation, tell your guests if they are not prequalified yet and want to be prequalified, you will have a mortgage company at the event. Invite them to bring any documents relating to prequalification so they can get a pre-qualification letter that same day.

- Add a Zoom link to invite more people who are unable to make it in person. Record just the important parts of the presentation to use in your social media. You can promote a live presentation in your social media if you desire.

- You can also have a virtual debut if you do not want to do one in person. The virtual debut of your new business can be at your broker's office, your home, or any office that supports you in your opening. You will invite only virtual guests and make it go live on several social networks at the same time. Everything will be the same: raffles, presentations, and especially guests will be registered with your information to receive gifts and sign up for additional services. Keep the duration to a maximum of an hour and a half instead of two hours. Be creative.

In a digital grand opening, you might do the prequalifications and property searches in Zoom breakout rooms or make appointments with the interested guests. Have a log or calendar on hand to make the appointments. Revise your agenda to allow the other sponsors to have time to present.

For example: A Saturday Grand Opening from 3:15 p.m. to 5:15 p.m.

Business Debut Timetable

Time	Activity	Sponsor	By:	Other
3:15-3:45 p.m.	Refreshments Raffle Referral Forms Raffle Tickets	Any mortgage company	Loan originator Any person	Have people for: tickets, referral forms, refreshments.
3:30-3:45 p.m.	PowerPoint presentation	*Optional if someone prepares the presentation for you	Any realtor Real estate agent, team	Get a big screen TV People sit & watch the presentation.
3:45-4:00 p.m.	Opening Guest speakers	ABC Realty Any title company Any mortgage company	Broker Title agent Loan originator	Max 3 people speaking for no more than 3-5 min; include the new agent's bio, achievements, etc.
4:00-4:15 p.m.	New agent speaks		New agent	Tell how you will help your clients, mention your team. Talk no more than 10 mins.
4:15-4:30 p.m.	Closing Guest Speaker New Agent	School of Real Estate	R.E. Instructor New Agent	Thanks to all for your support…
4:30-5:15 p.m.	Questions Prequalification Property Search Raffle, gifts, surprises	Any mortgage co Any realty co Any title co Real Estate Team New Agent School of RE	Loan originator R.E. broker Title agent Agent's team New agent Instructor	Have tables so you can help the guests separately. Have all tools for prequalification, search for properties, additional materials. Prepare for questions.

- If you wish, invite several companies (one of each: title company, mortgage broker, inspection service, appraiser, construction company, alarm system provider, etc.) to help you and collaborate in your business by becoming a team of professionals. These companies may be asked to bring something for the event such as refreshments or snacks, as well as information about their company. They will benefit from the exposure you provide. In addition, you could ask them to print marketing materials for you like postcards, invitations, flyers, or other items that might benefit you.

- Tell the companies you will be doing a raffle and they should bring whatever they want to give away, such as free services, a restaurant gift card, a Visa gift card, or a discount off services they provide. For example, a construction company could offer a voucher of $100 off repairs, paint, etc. Other companies like a real estate school could give a free course.

Be sure to invite these companies and people:

- Your real estate company
- Your team or partner if you have one or other agents if you want to work with them
- Mortgage company, title company
- Construction company, inspection company, appraisers.
- Alarm company, companies that guarantee the electrical equipment of a house (this is good for the homeowner to demonstrate they have when they sell)
- Home insurance company
- Developer in your area
- Other businesses that provide complementary services for homeowners. They will help you with referrals.

What You Could Say in Your Speech at the Opening

Example #1 of someone starting a new business

I want to take this opportunity to thank all of you for coming and supporting me in my new business. As you will see, I am serious about this business and I want to work for you and others who need my services to help you in selling, buying, or renting.

Whether it is selling your home, buying your dream home, or finding the right rental arrangement, my priority is the satisfaction of my clients. My team and I want to wow you with our professionalism and commitment.

I decided to start this wonderful business and learn more about buying and selling properties because I have loved real estate ever since I bought my first home. When I received my license, my goal was to always offer exceptional, excellent service and to listen to my customers' needs, to better help them and share information in the best way possible.

Acknowledgements to include as a new real estate agent:

Thank you (company name) and my broker (name of broker) for all the support you have given me and the support you give to my clients.

Thank you also to the team. We have more than 20 years of combined experience to serve you in all your needs.

Thank you again and enjoy everything!

I am (say your name) from (company name) here to help you in all your real estate projects!

Adapt the speech to make your presentation more comfortable. The speech above is only an idea and includes the most important points your new clients will need to consider before working with you.

Example 2: Debut of an agent with or without experience who never had a grand opening

I want to thank you all for sharing this special moment with me: the reopening of my business.

Some of you know, I have been in this business for/or since (you can include the years you have been in the business) and I've never done a grand opening, so I invited you to come to share that I'm here to serve you and let you know how important you are to me.

My greatest satisfaction and priority are to know that my clients and friends are fulfilled with the work and service I provide, and so you know there is a lot of love and professionalism in my business. This has always been my intention since entering the real-estate business, to always serve my clients. I want to thank my broker, company, and my team for getting me thus far.

I work with a team. Combined, we have more than 25 years of experience. We've provided quality service and professionalism. We also collaborate and lean on the experience of my broker (name of the broker whether present or virtually).

Again, thank you, and remember, whenever you or someone you know needs my services, please refer them to me. I will be eternally grateful.

Now, enjoy the party and talk with any of our experts to do a property search or run a comparable for your property. Feel free to ask any questions you have.

We have experts here today who can help you, as well as a mortgage company that can prequalify you today and give you a preapproval letter. All consultations are free and with no obligation.

This service is also for virtual guests. We will do the raffle; everyone should have one or more tickets depending on the number of referrals you provided. Zoom guests can participate (if that option was chosen on the referral sheet).

I am (say your name) from (company name), here to help you and thanks again for your support.

Raffle form

Welcome to the Business Debut of [Insert Logo]

Guest Information
Name:
Phone:
Email:
Address:
Referred by:
Homeowner? YES ☐   NO ☐   Wanting to rent? Yes ☐   No ☐ Looking for service? YES ☐   NO ☐ Tell me how I can help:

Receive a ticket for each referral you list. If you fill out all five referrals, you receive a gift!

Name	Phone	Email
1.		
2.		
3.		
4.		
5.		

This form is an example. Adapt it however you'd like. The most important thing is to get the information you need to contact the referral. Print, email, or post it to your website so people can sign up for your debut or for any other event you have.

The goal of your grand opening is to invite your contacts, neighbors, past customers, their references, and others to do business with you or provide their referrals. When you do this, you immediately multiply your clientele, which will be reflected in your income.

On this day, be prepared and have computers available. Mortgage companies can prequalify your clients, title companies can answer any guests' questions, and your broker and team can answer any questions of prospective clients. If you do not have a team, ask someone to help you as an assistant or team partner. You want to show prospects what your performance will look like when they're ready for your help. It's best to have all the support you need.

Offer the same services virtually if you can and use breakout rooms to allow prospects to have private conversations with you, the professional companies you invited, or your team. If you do not have a Zoom Pro account, ask your broker or a guest company to use their account, or subscribe to Zoom Pro for a month to use the upgraded features.

Record the event in parts. Example: record the opening, each company representative who will be giving an important message, and the farewell. Post these snippets of video on social media and embed them on your website to attract customers.

Important documents to have on grand opening day:

- Any printed material that lists your information (name, telephone, email, website, and company name). You could custom print pens, postcards, calendars, notebooks, calculators, or other goodies that your guests can take with them. Find a company online that will allow you to buy small amounts of printed swag at an affordable price.
- Have gift certificates printed. If they buy or sell a property with you, they will receive a benefit. This keeps your customers loyal, and they will come back to you when they need your services again. Example: If they sell their home with you, they will receive a voucher for $250 credit off their closing costs, or the cost of the appraisal of their property.
- At the venue entrance, have each guest who arrives sign into the guest book and list their complete contact information: their full name, address, whether they own a home or rent,

phone, email, free services they may need today, and comments. It is good to have this information, just in case the guest doesn't want to participate in the raffle. (They need to provide referral names if they want to be in the raffle. A portion of your guests will not be willing to give referrals. At least you will have their contact information.)

- After they sign the guest book, give them the referral signup. Encourage them to provide the names and contact information for one to five referrals. Have someone collect the referral sheets and give the guest an extra ticket for each referral they listed for more opportunities to win prizes. Whoever gives the most referrals automatically wins a prize, and anyone who lists at least five referrals gets a prize or give them double or triple tickets. It's important to promote the referral raffle because referrals are the key to expanding your business.

- Use a nametag for you, your team, and your broker and include the name of your company. If you do not have a printed nametag, buy nametag stickers and use them for each person at your company, including their title and company name.

- Choose your master of ceremonies in advance. This person will open the event, introduce you, and later wrap up the event. You can have guests speak if you wish, such as your broker or the mortgage company. Keep these talks brief since you want your guests to remember that you are the host and the reason for the event. If they talk, let them know beforehand they should emphasize you and your business, and to focus more on how the process works in collaboration with them. Limit their speaking time to no more than four minutes since people will be able to speak with them privately later.

- Mention the other companies and let guests know they can speak with them privately later, whether they visit their tables at the event in person or go to a virtual breakout room.

- Keep an agenda of how you want everything to happen during your grand opening. If your grand opening is virtual, it would be helpful to have a tech-savvy moderator to help with logistics so you don't have to worry and can focus on your business and guests.

Chapter 5

"ADHP"
Action, Discipline, Habit, and Passion!

First Step to Success: Act Today

The definition of action originates in the Latin vocabulary "actio." Action means you no longer have a passive role. It assumes dynamic change, additional facts that happen on the fly, and changing circumstances. Action is the ability for a person to change their activities to get a result.

People tend not to like any type of change, but *action* is the first step to success. When you want to improve or create a new habit, usually the hardest part is just getting started. It is the same way with a person who has not exercised. They first need to start the activity. Experts say you must spend **28 days** doing the same action to become disciplined. I would say spend a full month, **30 days minimum, and you will create the discipline.**

What actions should a real estate agent take? First determine which habits will result in the most clients. Start with one new habit, master it, then add another and another until your actions are in line with your goals and expectations.

Actions I Recommend

Prospecting

1. Action: Call every day or at least two to four days a week. Break it up into time blocks, one in the morning starting at 9:00 a.m., the second in the afternoon starting at 4:00 p.m. Each time block should last one to two hours.

2. Action: Post on social media, send private messages, use carousel posts, and post on You-Tube. Do your social media outreach when you're not working with clients directly or making your calls. You could advertise a new listing, whether it's yours or from another realtor (ask them for permission), do a video of yourself and talk about your services, post motivational pictures, and more. (Be creative.)

The two daily time blocks for making calls are essential to maintain your forward activity. As they become a discipline, you will have more appointments and will have a few days in which you can only call once a day. Be sure to keep your calling time in the morning as priority. This will keep you focused; in just 30 days, you will move from action to discipline.

Remember, while you are building your business, 80% of your time must be spent prospecting, while the remaining 20% is for the rest of your activities. For that simple reason, you must call every day. Place each time block on your agenda, then respect the time as if it were another appointment. You must give it the same priority.

It's the same thing with social media posting. Do at least one hour of social media outreach for two to four days a week or hire a person or a company to do this type of marketing. If you do not know, learn. Take classes by the board of realtors or at any school.

If you do not like social media, you must make more calls, approach more people, and do more follow up to get more referrals.

If someone asks you for an appointment at the same time as your call routine, try to schedule the appointment before or after your calling block. That is why having two time blocks for calling is helpful. If you are too busy, you always have another one left (the morning or afternoon call).

3. Action: Hand out a minimum of five business cards daily. Challenge yourself to not return home unless you have delivered a minimum of five business cards or send an email, text message, or social media message to five new people to promote your services.
4. Action: Send an email campaign or regular mail to your database according to how you have them organized. These could be groups of past customers, prospects, friends, family, referrals, or by zip code if you specialize in an area.
5. Action: Return all your calls within 24 hours.

In short, action is the most important thing you can do. It will lead you to achieve everything you want in life. Without action, you will not be able to move to the next level, **discipline.**

Second Step to Success: Create Discipline

Discipline is an individual's method, guide, and knowledge. It is linked to behavior and attitude. Self-discipline consists of various models and procedures to perform in an unwavering and relentless way. It becomes permanent and achieves the objectives that have been proposed.

As you adopt the new behaviors in the **Action** step, use self-discipline to continue these actions until you achieve permanent success. Here's how:

After you have performed your desired actions for 30 days, continue to do them an additional three months minimum. This cements the behavior, and you will have created positive and productive actions that will result in a lasting, thriving business. You're now ready to reach the next level: **habit.**

Discipline is the key to your business and is the difference between you being a successful agent or a mediocre one. Discipline is the key to your successful future. Lack of discipline means the destruction of your business. Being your own boss requires self-discipline. Without it, you will fail in this or any business you do.

To succeed at the highest levels in any profession will require discipline. Major league baseball players, world-class pianists, and highly-compensated salespeople all have the discipline they need to succeed in their field. When you were a child in school, what happened to the undisciplined children or those who didn't want to do homework or study? What was the result?

It is better to do one activity with discipline than to do several without. To flex your self-discipline muscle, try meditation. Sometimes the key to moving forward is to first quiet your body and mind.

Third Step to Success: Positive Habits

In Latin, "habitus" is a perception with various meanings. A habit could be a custom or routine that is achieved from repeating similar behaviors. They can be both created or inherited.

A habit can be for you or against you, so evaluate your current habits to eliminate negative and toxic habits and develop new, positive ones. Do this in the same way you would create new beliefs.

(Positive affirmations, repetition, and meditation.) Knowing what your habits are, evaluating whether you want to continue them, and creating new, positive habits will help you in your real estate business.

It is not easy to eliminate a habit, but it is easier to change one habit to another. When people stop smoking, they tend to gain weight. They've replaced their smoking habit by overeating. You can use this in your favor when you replace one habit with a better one. You can turn this into a game (play mind tricks, this time in your favor).

- Start your day by doing the most important thing first. This is a priority-based habit.
- Start your day off with positivity. For instance, have a nutritious breakfast and set yourself up for a more motivated and productive day.

Five Types of Habits

Physical: The body and its care. The opposite is neglect of the body. For example: a positive habit is to practice a sport or exercise; the opposite is not do any kind of exercise.

Emotional: Your emotional connection with your partner, friends, family, and associates. The opposite is a bad relationship with your family, friends, and associates. This relates to the mood, feelings, attitudes, and emotions. Example: how you express your love for others.

Social: Associated with the larger culture, customs, group, society, traditions, and behaviors. Social habits are behaviors you tend to do unconsciously and automatically. Example: you might say something without thinking such as, "Good morning" when you greet someone. A bad social habit is seeking attention by complaining, or not paying attention to your loved ones.

Morals: What you believe is right or wrong, your ethics, consequences, personal beliefs, and values. The opposite is negative morality against yourself or society.

Intellectual: Relates to self-improvement (continuous learning) and understanding, thinking rationally in stressful circumstances, and not giving up easily.

These five types of habits will help you if you use them well.

Example 1:

Physical habit: If you have ever been an athlete, you will remember what it feels like to compete. Remember the positive side of competition: it implies character, action, discipline, habit, and the desire to win. These attitudes form a starting point to create a new habit. Set a goal to get twice as many customers this month as you have in the past. This develops the *habit of competing with yourself to be better every day.*

Example 2:

Emotional habit: If you have ever worked for someone the normal eight hours a day, five days a week, you know the type of self-discipline this requires. Repeat this for your real estate business. If you work part-time, decide how many hours you are going to work and apply those hours to the 80/20 rule. In other words, if you work 20 hours a week on real estate, you spend 16 hours prospecting. This is the goal until you have a wide clientele, gradually leveling up, but you will never stop prospecting.

Apply this **emotional habit**, *affection-love-passion to your work to fall in love with your career.* If you do not apply affection-love-passion to your work, you will have to apply pain instead. Either of the two ways works, depending on which one makes you act. If you do not do your job well, you will feel pain. Compare this pain against how it feels when you are fired from a job. It's the same in your real estate business. If you don't perform your work well, you will not be able to afford your business or your lifestyle. Everything you could have done with your commission money will no longer be possible.

Example 3:

Social habits: Are critical in this business. If you are already a social person, great! If you are not, you will need to start going at least once a week to social places such as church, your children's school, or networking events. When you're out, hand out your business card and create new contacts. The way you dress must project professionalism, so you will have to dress appropriately and adopt that habit wherever you go. You never know where you will find a good client. If you apply the full circle of follow up with all your clients, you will have five references and the references of the references are never-ending.

Example 4:

Moral habit: What you think about is good or bad, so tell yourself it is bad to be static. Remind yourself it is very good to talk and hand out your business cards and share your info. You will have positive results when you call people daily. When you do not do your calls or any job you planned, you will know that it's bad, and this will help you push yourself.

Example 5:

Intellectual habit: Increase your knowledge and understanding. Create a study habit and be a good student. When you were in school, you knew it was a requirement to study, do projects, and to finish your homework. Repeat this intellectual habit by reading about your business every week, and apply the practice by calling every day, posting on social media, sending emails, and talking with whomever is within three feet of you. That is your daily assignment.

Habits are essential for this or any business you do. Remember, you are your own boss, and you need to know more about your habits and how you can use them in your favor. Take the following habit test to know which and how many benefit you and which harm you.

Questionnaire:

1. Do you have a habit regarding your health, body, skin, etc.? Yes_____ NO_____ What is it?

   _____

   _____

   How often do you do this health habit? _____

   How long have you had this habit? _____ Is it positive_____ or negative_____

2. Do you have any habits in your current job? Yes_____ NO_____ How many? _____

   What are they?

   _____

   _____

   Are they negative_____ or positive_____

3. Do you have any habits regarding your culture, customs, group, society, traditions, and behaviors? Yes_____ NO_____

    What are they?

    _____

    _____

    How long have you been doing these habits? _____ How often? _____

    Are these habits negative_____ or positive_____

4. Do you have a habit of evaluating what is right or wrong? Yes_____ NO_____ What is it?

    _____

    _____

    How long have you been doing this? _____ How often? _____

    Is it negative_____ or positive_____

5. Do you have any habits of reading, learning, or education? Yes_____ NO_____ What are they?

    _____

    _____

    How long have you been doing them? _____ How often do you do them? _____

    Are they negative_____ or positive_____

-   If out of the five questions, you have five positives: Congratulations! You have the tendency to create and move under highly positive habits. You achieve success easily and if you add a couple of new, productive real estate habits, you will be dynamite.
-   If out of five you have four positives: You are a highly balanced person; you know what is right and good for you. Analyze the one habit that is not helping you and change it to one that is productive for your business.

- If out of five you have three positives: You are on the edge. Your business is going well, but you know you can do better. You must change those two habits that are not helping you and change them today, so you can start seeing results. Be more analytical and purposeful before you start a habit.

- If out of five you have two positives: You are being less productive and are showing a negative trend. Evaluate and choose three habits you can change, stop, or start to set your life up for success.

- If out of five you have only one positive: You have not given up hope yet, but you must work on your thinking. Analyze and re-analyze the four habits that are most important to your growth in both your business and your personal life.

- If you do not have any positives: You must take a 180-degree turn to see change. Change your habits today, starting now. Only then will you break your bad habits. Review the previous chapters and do a self-analysis. If you know something does not work and you know the "something" is you, make the change now, and make the change big. It's better to suffer for a short time to change now than to suffer your whole life for not changing.

Once you know which habits you need to develop, focus on each one to analyze each question separately and create the foundations you need for success in this business. When you contemplate your mistakes, you will find the answers.

Each person is different. Creating a habit requires taking an action for 30 days minimum, then continuing the discipline for three months minimum. For the next six months, continue the habit. Soon you will no longer be able to live without performing that habit. It will culminate in a passion, and you will love what you have created.

The Fourth and Best Part: Passion for Your Business

Passion gives you an infinite energy. It helps you focus on one thing until you achieve it. It is born of the heart and manifested in the body as energy and joy. Passion will give you the power to overcome any obstacle in your life, career, or relationships.

Passion and love are key factors and ingredients for success. If you do not love what you do, it will be harder for you to spend long hours working or doing the tasks needed to achieve success.

You will not like some of the activities you do in your work. However, if you love your profession, realize you will either need to deal with them yourself or find another solution. For instance, you could hire an assistant or business partner to do what you don't like doing. Although your attitude can increase or decrease your passion, passion is also a way of thinking.

Following a business plan will increase your passion levels and the chances of success in your business. The passion you feel about your business is the result of the actions you took in your business over the last 30 days, then the discipline you developed over three months, then the habits you cultivated over the next six months. If you lack passion in your business, start by changing your activities for the next 30 days. This is one way to spark and cultivate your passion, and it is entirely within your control. *You* have the power to ignite passion, maintain passion, induce passion, and rediscover your passion. Discovering your passion is like turning on a light. You cannot live without light, and you cannot succeed without passion. It is like a loveless marriage; a marriage that does not cultivate passion will fail. Likewise, you must feed your business with love.

In your business, passion is like a car's engine. Just like you start your car daily, reignite your passion by reinventing and motivating yourself daily. You will not find any multi-million-dollar producers of real estate who aren't passionate, because without that ingredient, success would have been impossible for them.

Maintain and care for your passion just like you take care of anything else you love. You maintain it by internal motivations: your reasons, goals, and objectives. It is wise to read positive statements about your goals aloud every day.

Why should you read your goals, objectives, and affirmations aloud?

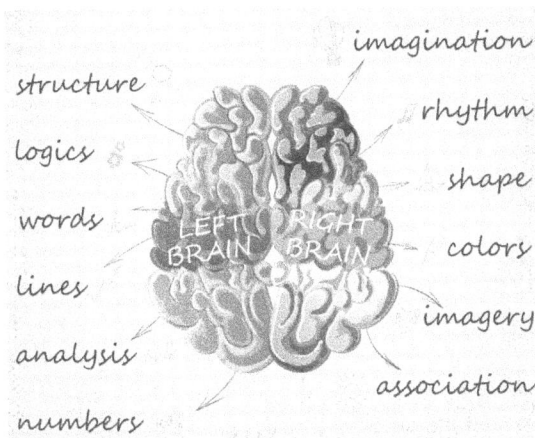

You learn in various ways: visual, tactile, kinesthetic, and auditory. For best results, learn how to activate them all. When you read aloud, you hear with your right ear, your artistic, emotional, motivational, and creative side. The left side is logical, rational, and analytical. When both ears hear what you say, the information will be unified, creating a perfect balance for the desired result.

In addition, by reading your affirmations aloud, you activate the muscle of the tongue that commands the brain that everything you say is fulfilled. Since this small and powerful muscle works miracles by sending messages to the brain to order what you ask it to do, be very careful what you repeat and say constantly, and especially what you say to yourself. The tongue is a powerful force for success or failure.

Achieve greater success by cultivating your actions, discipline, habits, and passion (ADHP).

When some people go into real estate, a mistake they make is to expect to have passion before they start their business. However, if you come into this business lacking passion, you need to know how to create it. It's like a woman going into labor; if it doesn't happen naturally, the doctor will induce it. This is your baby.

You can have success in whatever you set your mind to do. That is why you must learn how to increase your passion and motivation by repeating affirmations, goals, and objectives. You will have setbacks, and your superpower is to know how to get back up by reigniting your passion. Affirmations can help you do that.

If for some reason you do not do your affirmations one day, pick them up again the next day. Repeat this every day: "Today is my best day, the most important day of my life."

The Link of Customers and Passion

Your clients can tell if you love what you do. They prefer to work with an agent who has passion. They will be more excited to work with you and will remain loyal, becoming the best source of referrals who need your services. Clients notice the difference between working with a "dead" agent versus a working with a passionate + live + active = happy agent.

Questions that will keep your business fruitful and passionate:

1. How far have you come with respect to your real estate business?

_____

_____

_____

2. Where do you want to go?

_____

_____

_____

3. What do you think your customers want from you regarding your service?

_____

_____

_____

4. What do you think you have to learn to provide better service to your clients?

_____

_____

_____

5. Do you think you are passionate about your business? Yes_____ No_____

6. Do you think your clients know you love your business? Yes_____ No_____ Why?

_____

_____

_____

- When you have answered these questions, they will show you how to change your vision and enthusiasm for your business. They will help build your next career evolution.
- Challenges, when overcome, help build your enthusiasm, not destroy it. They build your confidence and knowledge to overcome the next set of challenges.
- The key to your success is discovering what motivates you. What fires you up?

- Feed the fire of your passion during the day. For example, if you feel tired or low energy in the middle of the afternoon, remember it's not important how many times you fall, but how many you get up. When athletes get tired, or have a setback during a game or practice, what do they do? They stop, breathe, recenter themselves by focusing on the task at hand, and start again. They do not give up or leave the game; they continue. That is what you should do too.

- Keep a reminder of what you're doing close at hand. It could be a card with the whys of your goal, objectives, and mission, or it could be an object that when you touch or see it, it reminds you of your vision. It could be a photo of your vision board, a stone, or a key to the house or car you want to buy. Whatever it is, keep it with you. It will help you immediately if you're attached by negative feelings. The faster your mood improves, the easier it will be to refocus on your goal.

Chapter 6

Real Estate Dictionary
Most Common Terms

A

Abandonment: Leave a property without leaving a successor. Voluntarily relinquishing rights of ownership.

Abatement: Reduction/decrease of payments on property taxes for a specific period.

Absentee Owner: Absent owner who does not live on the property.

Abstract of Title: A compilation of the records and history of the title of a property for all previous owners until the present.

Acceleration Clause: Clause in which the lender asks the buyer to pay the rest of the loan in full. Buyer is required to pay the debt earlier than the full term for breach of the agreement.

Acceptance: Voluntary agreement to an offer between all parties in the contract.

Accession: An increase in the property value for natural reasons such as a riparian right, etc.

Accretion: Increase of land mass due to deposits of soil from the movement of a lake or river.

Accrued items: Accumulated accounts, deferred accounts, expenses owed but not yet paid such as mortgage interest that is paid at the end of the month.

Acknowledgment: Attestation (written declaration). Formal statement in front of a notary or lawyer.

Acres: Measure of land equivalent to 43,560 square feet, 4,810 square yards, 4,047 square meters, 0.4047 hectares, 160 square rods.

Action to quiet title: Action to establish the validity of a title; action to gain full title.

Add Value Tax: According to value (Latin "by value"). Method of taxation for real estate properties. Tax payable every year.

Addendum: Used to add something to the contract like an extension of the closing date. It must be signed by all parties involved in the contract.

Adverse Possession: Possession without fair title by paying the taxes on the property. Possessing the property under certain conditions.

Affidavit of Title: Affidavit of ownership, written affidavit of the title of the property. Proof that sellers own the property.

Agency: Agency, management; agency law. Relationship in which one party represents the other like a listing agreement (agent represents the seller who is the principal).

Agency Coupled with an Interest: Agency coupled with an interest between the agent and the agency about a property. For example, a real estate broker agrees to work with a bank to do BPO (broker price opinion). In exchange, the broker will get listings from the bank.

Agent: Person who is authorized to represent the seller or the buyer in a real estate transaction as a real estate agent.

Air Lot: Block of space in the air. Right that can be transferred for consideration.

Air Rights: The rights to use the air space above properties. All rights. The air right can be used for several purposes.

Alienation: Transfer a property to another person. The alienation can be voluntary by the sale of a property or involuntary.

Alienation Clause: Disposal clause. A mortgage balance statement that says when the loan expires, the loan is paid immediately if the owner sells the property. Due on sale clause.

American Land Title Association Policy (ALTA): Policy of the U.S. Association of Title founded in 1907. Trade association that represents the title insurance industry.

Americans with Disabilities Act (ADA): Prohibits discrimination against people with disabilities in several areas such as employment, programs, services, etc.

Amortization: The installment payments of a loan that can be for several months or years.

Amortized Loan: Periodic payments in which payments are distributed between principal that helps reduce the debt, and interest that pays the cost of the loan.

Amount Realized on Sale: Amount the seller made in profit on the property. Profit from the sale of real estate.

Annexation: Any equipment or object joining or attaching to the property. For example, a microwave oven attached to the wall.

Annual Cap: The maximum interest rate a bank or lender can charge on a receivable in a one-year period.

Annual Percentage Rate: Annual interest rate, yearly interest rate of the loan.

Anti-Trust Law: Affects pricing, a statute that protects the consumer from predatory businesses and requires fair competition.

Anticipation: Valuation for future use on a property. Appraisal method that uses the principle of value for future use on a property, land.

Apportionment Clause: Delivery clause; Prorated clause of an insurance policy divided between policies depending on coverage.

Appraisal: An opinion of value based on the factual analysis of a property.

Appreciation: Rise, appreciation, price increase to the property for diverse reasons such as home improvements.

Appurtenant easement: An easement that passes from one property owner to the next upon the sale of the property. An appurtenant easement allows use of the property by a neighboring property, such as using their driveway.

Appurtenance: Deputy Right, accessory right that is transferred with the land, giving you the right to use the land of the neighbor's property.

Area: Zone, space. Surface space of a building or land.

ARM (Adjustable-Rate Mortgage): Mortgage with an interest rate that can be adjusted annually or semi-annually. The interest rate is based on the index.

Arrello-Association of Real Estate License Law officials: An organization of civil servants of national and international license law for the facilitation of exchange of ideas, cooperation, regulation, and real estate policies.

As Is: Without any warranty. The property is sold in the condition it currently is.

Asking Price: Price at which the seller wants to sell his or her property.

Assessment: Tax appraisal, taxation. Property estimated value for tax purposes on a property, and/or business.

Assessor: Appraiser, a local government official who determines the value of a property for tax purposes.

Assignment: Transfer of a legal document in writing.

Assumption of Mortgage: Assumable mortgage, all payments and title of the property go to the buyer. Usually, lender must approve of the arrangement to release the seller from liability.

Attachment: To add a debt to a property by a court order from the creditors.

Attorney-in-Fact: A person appointed to act for another person (principal). It is necessary to sign a power of attorney and this document needs to be signed and notarized.

Attorney's Opinion of Title: Written statement by an attorney regarding the title of the property.

Auctioneer: Person who coordinates an auction.

Automatic Extension: An extension clause added to some listing agreements, also known as an extender clause, to protect listing agents by guaranteeing their full commission after the listing expires in case a prospective buyer comes back after the expiration date.

Avulsion: Sudden move of the earth from one terrain to another because of flooding or when a river changes course.

B

Back Taxes: Taxes of a property that are not paid. The unpaid taxes could be partially unpaid or fully unpaid.

Backup Contract: A real estate contract that is put into effect when the previous contract fails. The contract is on hold and waiting.

Balance: The amount that a buyer must bring or wire at closing when purchasing a property.

Balloon Payment: A higher payment, substantially higher than monthly payments; a final total payment.

Bankruptcy: Economically broken. Could be voluntary (the person starts and ends the bankruptcy process) or involuntary bankruptcy (initiated by creditors).

Base Line: Demarcation base line that surveyors use in government surveys to create township lines.

Basis: Adjusted base value. Could start with the original investment amount in the property or amount of capital invested in the property.

Basis Point (BPS): Finance term meaning 1/100 of 1%, used to describe differences and changes in interest rate.

Beneficiary: The recipient of the trust or other income. The beneficiary can be an individual or bank (when it is a mortgage).

Biannual: Occurs twice in the year. Semiannual.

Bilateral Contract: Bilateral contract in which both parties (buyer and seller) must comply with the agreement.

Binder: Provisional safeguard for the purchase of a property. Report issued by a title company.

Blanket Loan: A loan that includes more than one property, and/or more than one loan. It is more common for developers than other property owners.

Blockbusting: Illegal practice of informing neighborhood homeowners about the arrival of certain groups of people to encourage them to sell at lower prices.

Blue-Sky Laws: State and federal laws governing the sale of securities and investments to protect investors from fraudulent sales of securities.

Blueprint: Group of dedicated plans for the construction of a building.

Board of Realtors: Local and/or national group of realtors associated for the benefit of all members. The board provides multiple tools, training, access to the MLS, and more for agents and brokers. This membership has an annual cost.

Book Value: Recent value of a property including the original asset cost minus depreciation.

Boot: A benefit given to compensate for the difference between two properties. When two properties exchange and one is worth more than the other, the difference must be compensated.

Branch office: An additional office location that is separate from the main office. Usually, branch offices are smaller than the main one.

Breach of Contract: Failure to perform the contract with no legal reason, either by the buyer or the seller. The breach could be partial or whole.

Broker: The licensed real estate broker operates an office and recruits agents. He or she must be an officer of a real estate office to be the designated principal broker.

Broker Associate: Broker sales associate. They are brokers but act as sales associates because if they don't open a brokerage, they must have their license with another broker who has a real estate company.

Broker Price Opinion: Opinion of value of the property based on the current market value. Like a CMA (Comparable Market Analysis). Can be done by a real estate broker, real estate agent, or an appraiser.

Broker Protection Clause: A clause granting the realtor compensation in case the sales contract expires and a client comes back later. The clause stipulates the timeframe. Also known as extender clause.

Broker-Salesperson: An agent who has a broker's license but chooses to work under another broker.

Brokerage: A real estate company that conducts real estate transactions for a commission and represents both parties in the transaction: the buyer and seller or landlord and tenant.

Buffer Zone: Intermediate zone that separates one parcel of land from another parcel of land.

Building: A structure, a shelter built for people, animals, or goods.

Building Code: Building rules for the protection of the public.

Building Line: Construction line to limit construction to certain boundaries that construction will not cross.

Building Permit: Permit given by a local government for the right to build, such as building a house, making home improvements, or developing land.

Bundle of Legal Rights: Set of legal rights of an owner on a piece of land.

Business Cycle: The cycle in the real estate industry and economy in a country or worldwide. The business cycles are expansion, recession, depression, and reactivation.

Buydown: Discounting interest on a debt to lower the monthly fee for a specific time, usually at closing before the first mortgage payment, before closing the sale.

Buyer-Agency Agreement: Agency agreement between the buyer and the agent or broker to represent the buyer in the purchase of a property.

Buyer Broker: The realtor represents the buyer in a real estate transaction.

Buyer's Market: Market in favor of the buyer, situation in which the buyer has more options when buying. There is more supply (properties for sale) than buyers.

By-laws: Statutes. Rules and regulations by associations or businesses that must be followed. Bylaws must be given to the buyer before buying a property within three business days if the property is a resale condo or fifteen days if it's a new condo.

C

Cancellation Clause: This clause allows the buyer or seller to cancel the contract for some specified reason granted in the contract.

Capital Gain: Gains realized after a sale. A capital gain is the difference between the sale price of a property minus the original purchase cost minus any other costs incurred related to the property.

Capitalization: An estimate for how much a property will return in income. Divide the property's net operating income by the current market value.

Capitalization Rate (Cap Rate): The expected rate of return of an asset. Used by investors to know if they invest in a specific property what is the rate of capitalization in the possible investment and what is the value of an income property.

Capitalization Recapture: The return on an investment that an investor desires to get plus the recapture of the initial investment, expressed by depreciation over the economic life of the asset.

Cash Flow: The cash flow of an individual, income property, or company. Can be positive or negative. Shows a gain or loss of value of the investment after all expenses are incurred.

Cash Flow Analysis: How a business generates cash, liquidity in a certain time frame.

Cash Rent: Rent received in cash, also a term used in farm rent to differentiate rent from crop income.

Caveat Emptor: Latin word meaning "let the buyer beware." When a buyer is purchasing a property, they assume risks in the quality and condition of the property.

Census Tract: A specific geographic area used in a census to gather demographic information containing data about income and population to create programs for people like schooling and more.

Certificate of Reasonable Value (CRV): Used in VA loans to determine the maximum allowed value of a loan for a property.

Certificate of Redemption: An official acknowledgment that the property owner has paid off all debts including property tax.

Certificate of Sale: Issued by the court and given to the winning bidder after buying the tax certificates of a property.

Certificate of Title: (Title of Ownership). A written opinion by an abstract attorney about the history and chain of title ownership of a property.

Chain of Title: Title history of a property from the first owner to the current one.

Change: The principle that no physical or economic condition remains static. For example, property prices are changeable and depend on supply and demand.

Channeling: The illegal practice by some agents of directing certain people to buy in specific areas because they are minorities.

Civil Rights Act of 1866: First law created to define citizenship; states that all people born in the U.S. have the same rights.

Clear Title: Free and clear of encumbrances; a free title without any lien or levy.

Client: The person agents and brokers work with in a real estate transaction, also known as customers, buyers, sellers, tenants, landlords, or principals.

Closing: Closing of a property, the consummation of a sale.

Closing Costs: Expenses that a person or entity must pay when buying or selling a property like points, an appraisal, a title policy, etc.

Closing Statement: An accounting document that details all the costs of the transaction, and the debits and credits in a closing transaction.

Cloud on Title: A doubt about the title that is discovered when doing a title search that must be clarified and solved before closing.

Clustering: Construction density. The lots where structures are built are smaller than normal to allow more open green space for the community.

Coastal Zone: Boundaries between the land and water.

Code: A comprehensive set of laws. They include criminal codes and building codes.

Code of Ethics: A set of values that organizations create to set up standards for what is right or wrong or correct to do in the business. For example, the code of ethics for realtors guides realtors to act respectfully and honestly.

Codicil: An addition to the will that modifies, explains, or revokes it.

Coinsurance Clause: Insurance company requires property owners to have an appropriate amount of insurance on their property and have a fair premium for the risk.

Color of Title: An apparent title that contains defects such as an incorrect recording of the name of the owner.

Commercial Broker: Agent that lists and sells commercial properties such as shopping malls, buildings, etc.

Commingling: Mixing of funds. For example, escrow accounts containing client funds should not be mixed with the personal funds or operating funds of the broker.

Commission: Commission that a broker/agent earns for their work representing either the buyer, seller, or both. The commission can be a percentage of the sale of the property, a flat fee, or a net amount the seller wants to pay. In addition, whatever the listing agent adds to the value of the property can become the commission.

Common Areas: Areas owned and used by all the people who live in a condominium, subdivision, etc.

Common Elements: Common property that people living in the condominium share among the owners of a building. Condominium property that is shared between owners could include a laundry area, park, or pool.

Common Law: Also known as case law. A body of law arising in customs, uses, and decisions in courts. (The term originated in England.)

Community Property: Joint property between married partners that was acquired while they were married.

Community Property Right of Survivorship: Two spouses equally share assets through marriage, and when one spouse dies all assets pass to the surviving spouse without going through probate.

Community Reinvestment Act: Federal law enacted in 1977 that encourages banks to reinvest in the credit needs of the community where they are located, including low- to medium-income communities.

Comparable: Market study of the value of properties that are similar to the property that is for sale.

Comparable Market Analysis (CMA): A report created by a real estate agent/broker to determine the value of a property. Shown to the seller in a listing presentation. The comparable report shows active listings, pending listings, and sold properties to get an estimate of fair market value of the seller's property.

Competition: Agents present information to buyers or sellers about the competitiveness of a price compared to other properties in the area. Also refers to competition between brokerages in services and to recruit agents.

Competitive Market Analysis: Summary of the technologies, commission, and services provided to the client that differentiates the agent from other agents in the area.

Compound Interest: Interest earned on the reinvestment of interest. Reinvesting real estate gains into another property or investment.

Condemnation: The legal process of expropriation by a government institution of a property for public use by compensating the owner.

Condition Precedent: A condition that says until everything in the contract is fulfilled, the agreement does not go into effect.

Condition Subsequent: A condition that takes effect after the agreement that the lender could ask the buyer to do, such as pay off credit card balances or repair something on the property.

Conditional-use Permit: Permission to use the property in a non-conforming way. Is considered an exception to the regular zoning process and allows the owner to use their property in a way that is different from others in the area.

Conditions: A set of requirements a bank or lender asks a buyer to do to close the loan. Example: providing income tax documents, or a letter of explanation for something in the buyer's credit report.

Condominium: A structure of more than two units that shares common areas between the owners.

Confession of Judgment Clause: A break-in clause allowing a judgment to be recorded in favor of the creditor and against the debtor without having to make a legal judgment on the part of the creditor.

Conformity: Compliance, similarity in an evaluation, giving a better value among the properties in the area.

Consideration: A form of value that a buyer gives as collateral to support the purchase of a property, such as money, services, or products.

Contingency: Something additional in a contract that must first be done to make it effective. For example, a loan might be contingent upon an inspection.

Constructive Eviction: Implicit eviction; ending a lease early without any future income liability due to a serious inconvenience created by the landlord.

Constructive Notice: Unlike actual notice, constructive notice says the notification happened, even if the person notified didn't receive the information.

Consulting: The act of providing information and giving advice related to real estate. Example: a real estate consultant.

Contract: An agreement, a legal document between two or more people or entities (buyer and seller, broker and client) that creates any type of relationship. Agreement between all parties to fulfill a promise, the agreement could be oral, written, or partially written.

Contribution: On some purchase contracts given from one party to another such as a gift or donation. The gift or contribution could be from a seller or from the buyer's side like a family gift. Also, the amount of increased value of a property when an improvement is made (not the cost of the improvement).

Conventional Loan: Considered a conventional mortgage, this loan could be conforming (using a lower interest rate and down payment such as 3%, 5%, 10%-20% down) or nonconforming (higher interest rate and down payment, mostly used on condos, hotels, investments, or with buyers with some qualification deficiencies). A conventional loan is not backed by the government.

Conveyance: Assignment or transfer of rights from one person or entity to another.

Cooperating Broker: A broker or agent who decides to share or split their real estate commission with another broker. Example: When a listing agent inputs a property for sale on the MLS, they are cooperating with other agents.

Cooperative (co-op): A group that exists in a building made up of the owners who are all shareholders. A form of real estate ownership where the owner purchases an interest in the corporation that owns the property as a shareholder.

Co-ownership: Two or more owners who each has a stake in the property.

Corporation: Group of people authorized to act as a single entity. Could be a C or S corporation, for profit, or a nonprofit corporation.

Corporeal Right: Tangible right to a property that can be touched, like a building, land, or house.

Correction Lines: Lines that correct for the curvature of the earth every 24 miles.

Co-signer: A person who is responsible for repaying the loan when the signer doesn't. Some banks require a co-signer if the person who applies does not qualify for credit by themselves, such as a new borrower without credit history.

Cost Approach: A way of computing the value of a property. The value would be land, plus total costs of construction, less depreciation.

Cost Recovery: Recovery of the initial cost of an asset through depreciation, amortization, or depletion.

Counteroffer: When one of the parties (buyer or seller) disagrees with the offer and decides to make another offer. This person becomes the offeror.

Covenant: Written agreement between both parties.

Covenant of Quiet Enjoyment: Usually inserted in a lease to allow the buyer use of the premises in peace without being evicted by someone with a superior title.

Credit: In a closing statement, the amount of money due to either a buyer or seller. Considered a receivable.

Current Eviction: Removal of a tenant, effective eviction.

Current Notice: Effective notification, something that is already known.

Curtesy: The right of a husband to receive his wife's estate and property upon her death.

Custom Builder: Unique house construction; each property has a unique design.

D

Damages: Recovery money for the suffered party. For example, if someone does not fulfill a contract, the deposit can be used to pay for those damages.

Date of Closing (Closing Date): When the transaction is executed and officially complete.

Datum: Reference horizontal line that measures height and depth.

Debit: A charge deducted in the closing of a transaction. Money that the buyer or seller owes at closing and will be deducted from proceeds (seller) or charged (buyer).

Debt: An obligation to pay. An amount due to someone else (bank, entity, or person)

Decedent: A person who is dead.

Dedication: Property that is voluntarily transferred by an owner to the public, with the assumption that the land will be used for public purposes.

Deed: Transfer of a property from a seller to a buyer.

Deed in Lieu of Foreclosure: The homeowner voluntarily signs over their property to the lender instead of going through the foreclosure process.

Deed of Trust: Agreement that the buyer will pay the loan and the lender will hold the title until the loan is paid.

Deed Restrictions: Limits how the property can be used in the future.

Default: Violation of an agreement for not performing.

Defeasance Clause: A clause that cancels the debt of a mortgage or lease when the payment conditions are satisfied.

Defeasible Fee Estate: Rights of ownership are contingent upon some contingency being performed or not performed. Full resolution domain.

Defect in Title: Defect in the title of a property that prevents the title agent from giving a clear, clean title.

Deficiency Judgment: Debt not covered by the sale of the property that secured the loan. There is a mortgage deficiency as it was sold below the balance. The lender can collect additional money to make up the balance.

Delivery and Acceptance: The transfer of the title of a property from one owner to another; this document must be signed and dated by all parties involved.

Demand: The number of buyers in a market compared to the number of properties for sale. Demand from the bank to pay a loan. An act of demanding.

Density Zoning: Specifies the maximum number of homes that can be built in a specific area.

Department of Housing and Urban Development (HUD): Federal agency in charge of housing needs and community development.

Deposit: Amount of money to set aside a property as a sign of interest in buying or renting it.

Depreciated Cost: Decline of the value of an asset over a set period.

Depreciation: Depreciation is given for the use, deterioration, and expected life of a property. It is tax deductible. Residential depreciation is 27.5 years, and commercial depreciation is for 39 years.

Depreciation Method: A method of depreciation that accountants use to decrease the value of a rental property. Method of depreciation: straight-line, double-declining balance, unit of production, and sum of years.

Descent: The succession of inheritance in the absence of a will.

Developer: Constructor, builder. Company that develops and constructs properties, buildings, lots, etc.

Devise: A legacy, the gift of a property through a will.

Devisee: The one who inherits a property through a will.

Devisor: The one who donates or gives the property through a will.

Discount Points: A fee the lender charges to reduce the monthly payments based on a lower interest rate. Known as buying down the rates. Some buyers buy discount points to pay less in their monthly payments. Every point of the loan is equal to a reduction of one eighth of the interest rate.

Discount Rate: Method used by lenders to determine the current value of future cash flow from a property.

Discounted Loan: Discount on the loan for less value. Buyers pay extra costs at closing to get a discount on their loan, like discount points.

Distraint: Legal right that an owner can seize a tenant's property until the tenant pays the late rent.

Distressed Property: Refers to property that is under foreclosure, pre-foreclosure or under the control of the lender. Could happen for diverse reasons such as defaulting on mortgage payments, property taxes, or being late on association fees.

Distressed Sale: When a seller must sell their property so they do not go bankrupt or have a mortgage judgment against them.

Doctrine of Relation Back: Legal doctrine of retroactive effect. For example, when a buyer gives an initial deposit, the deposit is dated as of the day it was received and not when the property closes.

Documentary Transfer Tax: A tax that applies to properties when they transfer to new ownership.

Dominant Tenement: A dominant property allows the owner to have an easement on another property, considered the servient tenement, for access to specified resources.

Double Taxation: Pay twice in taxes for the same income. For example, a "C" corporation has double taxation, first on its own profits, then its investors are taxed when they receive dividends.

Dower: Gives a wife the right to keep her husband's property upon his death.

Down Payment: Amount one pays for the property in addition to the debt.

Dual Agency: Double Agency. When an agent or broker represents both the buyer and seller in a real estate transaction. It is illegal in Florida.

Due-on-Sale-Clause: When a property is sold, the clause states the mortgage balance must be paid in full.

Duplex: Two units under the same roof with two separate entrances.

Duress: Coercion. To force someone to agree to a contract. This is illegal and invalid.

Dwelling: Place of residence, such as house, condo, etc.

E

Earnest Money: Security deposit to buy a property, applied as a credit at closing. If the buyer does not comply with the terms of the contract, the buyer could lose the deposit.

Easement: Grants access to a property for certain purposes such as a utility easement, access to a main road, etc.

Easement by Appurtenant: Right to cross another person's property to access your property.

Easement by Condemnation: The government can use condemnation of a property to claim eminent domain and seize it if it's needed for public use purposes such as roads, airports, powerlines, etc.

Easement by Implication: When a property is divided, it's possible to claim prior use and gain access if it's reasonably necessary. For example, if the divided property now blocks the access of the parcel in the back.

Easement by Necessity: An easement necessary to allow the landowner to access their property. Without the easement (granted by law, not agreement), their property would otherwise have no access to a street or highway.

Easement by Prescription: Prescription Bondage. Created when an individual repetitively uses part of the other owner's property without permission.

Easement in Gross: Selling the rights to land without giving them legal ownership. For example, the electric company might have an easement to run a power line across a property.

Economic Base: Industry within the geographic market area that provides job opportunities needed for the community.

Economic Life: Life of a property. In real estate, the number of years the property may be profitable.

Economic Rent: The amount of rent that exceeds what is necessary to justify the investment.

Effective Gross Income: Potential gross income from all sources of revenue in an income property except vacancy and non-payment by renters (collections costs).

Efficiency Unit: Small unit usually in a house where the owner converted a garage into an efficiency apartment that contains a bathroom and has a private entrance. An efficiency apartment has all the functionality of multiple rooms in one: bedroom, living room, and kitchen. Same as a studio apartment.

Ejectment: Removing someone from a property who has no rental contract (they are not a tenant).

Emblements: Fruits of the earth, harvest. The harvest belongs to the tenant who cultivated the land, regardless of who has possession at the time of harvest.

Eminent Domain: Expropriation of a home by the government for public use.

Employee: A person who works for an employer and is hired to do a job. They are paid by a salary or hourly rate. At the end of the year, they receive a W-2 form from their employer which summarizes their income, taxes, and other information for the year.

Employment Contract: Agreement between an employee and employer or an independent contractor like an agent or broker.

Enabling Acts: Laws and entities that create, regulate, and authorize zoning of property within their jurisdictions.

Encroachment: Invasion of one property owner onto another property. Could be intentional or unintentional and could include pouring concrete or constructing a fence or wall that extends into their neighbor's property.

Encumbrance: Lien or claim against a property that somehow diminishes the value or use of the property. Could make it more difficult to sell.

Entity: Form of ownership in a property. A company is an entity.

Entrepreneur: An individual who starts and maintains a business activity and takes risks.

Environmental Impact Report: A report of the environmental impact of development in an area to know what consequences that development might have on the environment.

Equal Credit Opportunity Act (ECOA): Equal opportunity to obtain credit for all individuals without discrimination.

Equalization: The rate between counties for the purpose of valuing property taxes. Ensures that taxpayers pay their fair share compared to each other.

Equalization Factor: To calculate property taxes, the state equalizes the value of properties across the state by multiplying a percentage against the value of the property.

Equitable Lien: An enforceable lien levied by the court to achieve fairness. For example, it might be used when one party improves the real estate of another person.

Equitable Right of Redemption: Right to pay off a mortgage lien and all costs associated with it to stop the foreclosure of a property.

Equitable Title: Right of possession. For example, an investor may hold an equitable title but not the legal title. They may enjoy the benefits of the property without having legal title to it.

Equity: Difference between the current value of the property and the principal balance of the debt on the property.

Erosion: Water or wind wear away the land; movement of soil off the property due to natural causes.

Escalation Clause: An adjustment clause in which lease payments gradually increase based on the consumer index. Also, in a contract, the buyer can include an escalation clause that states they will pay a higher price for a property if the seller receives a higher bid.

Escheat: The property is reverted to the state when there are no heirs to the property, or the property is unclaimed.

Escrow: Security deposit during a sales or rental transaction that is usually held by a third party such as an attorney, title company, or in a real estate escrow account.

Escrow Account: Bank account separate from the operating account that is used exclusively for holding escrow deposit transactions like sales and/or leases.

Escrow Agent: A licensed title agent, attorney, or another neutral third party who holds the funds during the closing of a real estate transaction until both parties have fulfilled their obligations.

Escrow Instructions: Instructions for the deposit requirements and custody instructions. Written directions to an escrow agent containing various information such as the bank name, buyer and seller information, and more.

Estate in Land: The interest a person has in real property; they are or may become the owner in the property.

Estate Taxes: Federal taxes on the transferred estate of a deceased person.

Estate/Tenancy at Sufferance: Possession of a rental property after the lease agreement has expired, without a new lease or renewal of the lease but under the previous lease's terms.

Estate/Tenancy at Will: Possession at will; indefinite term of rent until one of the parties decides to terminate.

Estate/Tenancy for Years: A time-defined lease that grants possession and terminates automatically at the end date.

Estate/Tenancy from Period to Period: Possession of a property that automatically renews after a specific period: weekly, monthly, or annually.

Estoppel: A signed statement that says certain facts are correct.

Estoppel Certificate, Estoppel Letter: A signed statement of facts that can't be later contradicted. If a landlord needs to establish certain facts with a third party, they might need an Estoppel Certificate from the tenant that verifies lease terms and conditions. In HOA communities, the HOA may be asked to provide the estoppel letter, verifying HOA dues and rules. Used as part of due diligence in many real estate activities.

Ethics: Rules and codes of conduct that guide professionals as to what is right or wrong. Example: the code of ethics for realtors.

Eviction: Legally dislodge a tenant from a property.

Evidence of Title: In writing, proof of ownership such as a deed that proves who owns the property.

Exchange: Interchange, a swap of property held for investment purposes. It has tax advantages. For example, the 1031 exchange allows a person or entity to sell their property, then buy another property within a specific time at a similar price and type ("like-kind"). The capital gain is deferred.

Exclusive-Agency Listing: The seller pays only when the agent sells the property. If the seller finds the buyer, they do not pay the agent a commission.

Exclusive Right-to-sell-listing: An agreement between the seller and the broker to sell his/her property for a flat fee or commission. Since it's exclusive, the seller agrees to pay the listing broker a commission, regardless of who sells the property.

Executed Contract: Fulfilled, both parties have complied with the terms of the agreement.

Execution: When all parties in the contract sign, initial, and date the contract, and fulfill the obligations they promised in the contract.

Executory Contract: Contract that has not been fully completed, either by the buyer or seller. A contract that has unperformed obligations.

Express Agency: An agency created between the party and the agent; could be written or oral.

Express Agreement: When both parties express what they want in the agreement; could be written or oral.

Extension: Agreement between two parties to extend a contract for diverse reasons such the need for securing financing, more time to clear the title, etc. The contract would have new deadlines for completing tasks.

External Depreciation: Depreciation of the property by external means. Example: a change in price because of changes in supply and demand.

External Obsolescence: Environmental obsolescence. Could be due to location, economics, or social forces. The owner cannot recouperate the loss in value by spending money to fix the property.

F

Facade: Wall on the outside front of a building. The main face of the building.

Face Amount: Dollar value shown in the contract in numbers or words. The original loan amount.

Fair Housing Act: The Equality Act governs everything related to the acquisition of homes; prohibits discrimination in housing based on race, color, religion, national origin, sex, family status, and disability.

Fannie Mae: Federal National Mortgage Association (FNMA). Founded in the United States in 1938 during the Great Depression, the government-sponsored enterprise. Since 1968, a publicly traded company.

Farm Service Agency: Administration agency for rural economic and community development that provides loans to farmers and those living in rural areas.

Farming: Marketing and strategic technique used by listing agents to position themselves as the expert resource in a particular neighborhood or demographic. Agents mail letters and postcards and advertise in the neighborhood in other ways.

Federal Deposit Insurance Corporation (FDIC): A United States government corporation that provides deposit insurance against losses in banking institutions; guarantees the safety of deposits up to $100,000 in a bank.

Federal Home Loan Mortgage Corporation (FHLMC): Known as Freddie Mac, a private corporation founded by Congress that helps to promote affordability in home ownership.

Federal National Mortgage Association (FNMA): This organization purchases mortgages from different lending institutions to help increase affordable lending options that lending companies can offer.

Federal Reserve System: The central banking system of the United States. Created on December 23, 1913 to help support the economy.

Fee Simple Absolute: Full absolute ownership. Synonymous with ownership, a freehold ownership, and inheritable.

Fee Simple Subject to Condition Subsequent: Fee simple, but subject to a condition. If a specific future event happens, the grantor will get the fee simple back (or power of termination).

Feudal System: Associated with England. The sovereign owns all land and properties within the kingdom, and grants use of the land to his vassals, tenants, and others based on loyalty to the crown as a reward for service or labor. When the person dies, the land could pass not to their heirs but back to the sovereign.

Fiduciary: A trustee, a trusted person who holds a legal or ethical relationship. Could be a person, group of people, or a company. In real estate, a real estate agent who represents a principal.

Fiduciary Relationship: When someone places complete trust and confidence in another person to act in their interest.

Fifteen-year mortgage: Loan amortized to fifteen years at a fixed rate. It amortizes in 180 months.

Financial Institutions Reform, Recovery and Enforcement Act 1989 (FIRREA): United States federal law for reforming, recovery, and the enforcement of financial institutions after the savings and loan crisis of the 1980s.

Financial Statement: A financial statement demonstrating the income, expenses, and debt of a person or institution.

Financing: A loan. How a buyer secures funds for a real estate transaction.

Fiscal Policy: How the government will tax and spend money.

Fixture: Items permanently attached to the property.

FHA 203(K): Federal loan program that finances the purchase of and repairs to a house.

FHA Loan: Federal Housing Administration. Helps buyers purchase a home with a minimum down payment of 3.5%. A buyer can only have one FHA loan at a time.

Flood Insurance: Insurance that covers potential flooding on a property. It is required if the property is in a flood zone and optional if it's not in a flood zone.

Foreclosure: A mortgage judgment against the borrower. Legal process where the bank takes ownership of the property and tries to sell it to recover the cost of the loan.

Foreclosure Sale: When a bank exercises its lien right and sells a property at auction. The sale of a property to satisfy a mortgage debt.

Form 1099: Federal tax form used in a property sale to record proceeds from real estate transactions for capital gains. Also refers to the form individuals receive when working as independent contractors to report non-job income.

Fractional Section: Land or lot less than 160 acres.

Franchise: Allows the franchise name to be used for a fee or as a commission of the sale or transaction. Each franchise owner owns their own agency and pays a percentage of the gross income of each. Franchise examples: Century 21, Keller Williams, Remax, etc.

Fraud: When a person obtains money or any other asset in a wrongful way.

Freehold Estate: Ownership of a property for an indefinite period. Right of title to land.

Front Footage: A measurement of the amount of property that is contiguous to the street or public right-of-way.

FSBO (For Sale by Owner): A property that is for sale by the owner. The owner does not have a real estate agent and is representing himself/herself in the sale of his/her property.

Functional Obsolescence: An improvement that causes the property to lose value due to its age or an outdated design.

Future Interest: An interest in a property that occurs in the future. This right is not in the present.

FY Fiscal Year: A twelve-month period usually from January 1-December 31 to report business operations to the IRS.

G

GAAP-Generally Accepted Accounting Principles: The income tax basis of accounting required for public companies.

Gap: A defect in the title string of a property.

Gated Community: A community of properties that is usually walled off and accessed only by strictly controlled entrances.

General Agent: A general agent can represent any or all acts of the principal. The principal can have several general agents and decide what type of work each will do.

General Lien: A lien on all property, both real and personal, including clothing, furniture, real estate, etc. that can be sold to satisfy the debt.

General Warrantee Deed: The most used deed in a real estate transaction, written with a general title guarantee.

Gift Deed: Gift of property transferred voluntarily from one party to another.

Good Faith: The concept of honesty, to do something with good intentions.

Good Faith Estimate (GFE): The form used before 2015 that required banks to describe all closing costs for the buyer and seller.

Government Check: Government review that imposes square measures (576 square miles) on plots and municipalities used in the legal description.

Government Lot: A section next to water or another boundary which could have some irregularities in the lot and block measure.

Government National Mortgage Association (GNMA): Is a government-owned corporation of the United States within the department of HUD (Department of Housing and Urban Development).

Grant: Transfer of interest in a real estate property. Agreement to give something.

Grantee: Receiver (person who receives the grant). Generally, the receiver/grantee is the buyer.

Granting Clause: Property rights transfer clause that specifies the grantee's rights.

Grantor: The one who gives and makes a grant conveyance of the property rights.

Gross Income Multiplier (GIM): Used to calculate an estimated value of a rental property by dividing the property sales price by its gross annual rental income.

Gross Lease: A type of commercial lease where the rent includes all or part of the property's expenses such as taxes, insurance, utility, repairs, etc.

Gross Rent Multiplier (GRM): A ratio comparing the price of a real estate investment against the annual rental income before expenses like property insurance, property taxes, etc. GRM= Sales price divided by gross rent.

Ground Rent: Rental agreement between a landlord and tenant for the use of land. Most common in Pennsylvania and Maryland.

Ground Lease: Commercial lease of a piece of land in which the tenant develops the piece of property, usually for a longer term. It is typically a net lease.

Guaranty: Warranty. An agreement that guarantees a debt. A written guaranty.

Guardian: Individual appointed by the court to manage someone's assets if they are not able to perform (could be disabled or a minor).

H

Habendum Clause: Clause determining the transfer of ownership and extension of restrictions transferred. "To have and to hold" is known as the habendum clause.

Half Bath: Bathroom that has only a toilet and a sink, not a shower or bathtub.

Handyman's Special: Property that needs many repairs. These properties can be attractive for investors because they are usually cheaper than properties in good condition. Realtors write "handyman special" or use words related to handyman in their remarks on the MLS.

Hazard Insurance: Insurance that covers a property owner against catastrophes, damages, or accidents.

Hedge Fund: Group of investors who raise capital and invest it in real estate. Real estate hedge funds tend to invest in publicly traded REITs (Real Estate Investment Trust).

Heir: The successor of property by law without needing a will.

HELOC (Home Equity Line of Credit): Credit line using the equity in a real estate property. It is a revolving debt.

Hereditaments: Goods to be inherited; could be any type of personal property or real estate property capable of being an inheritance.

High-Rise: A tall building (a height more than six floors); the building could be residential or commercial.

Highest and Best Offer: When there are multiples offers on a property, the listing agent and seller choose the buyer who offers the highest price and best qualified offer compared to other buyers for the same property.

Highest and Best Use (HBU): Best use of the land or property that provides the best income return, the maximum benefit.

Holdover Tenancy: After the lease expires, the tenant continues to live on the property with the landlord's consent, paying the same rent as already stipulated in the previous agreement.

Holographic Will: Also known an oleographic testament. A will handwritten and signed by the testator without the services of a lawyer. Florida does not recognize holographic will.

Home Equity Loan: A type of loan that a borrower makes using the equity of the property as a collateral.

Home Inspector: Property Inspector. A licensed inspector who inspects a property before the sale to verify the conditions of the property.

Home Mortgage Disclosure Act: (HMDA). Federal law established in 1975 by Congress. The act requires lenders to keep records of loans and other information regarding the borrowers and provide the data to the public.

Homeowner's Insurance Policy: An insurance policy for a homeowner to protect their property from natural disasters, losses, liabilities, etc.

Homestead: The primary family residence. Applying for a homestead exemption can have several benefits such as a tax exemption. Also limits the annual increase of tax payments on the property each year to 3% per year maximum.

Housing and Urban Development Department (HUD): HUD is a major housing program, providing development assistance, support, and improving communities in conjunction with FHA programs.

I

Implied Agency: Agency that is created by conduct and circumstances and not by a written agreement between the principal and agent.

Implied Agreement: A contract that is created by the actions demonstrated by the parties involved. It is not written or spoken; it is assumed based on the actions and conduct of the buyer and seller, landlord and tenant.

Implied Contract: See implied agreement.

Implied Warranty of Habitability: Implicit guarantee of habitability in the property; requires landlords to keep the property in habitable condition.

Improved Land: Improved land either by adding utilities or something extra on-site or/an off-site land improvement. The improvement could be a building or any other type of upgrade.

Improvement: Any type of development of the land or the structure on it that increases the value of the property.

Income Approach: Method of estimating the value of properties that generate income such as shopping centers, buildings, hotels, etc. It is calculated annually by determining the net property income and dividing this number by the capitalization rate.

Incorporate right: Incorporeal law, right of way in another property for bondage use. Rights to property that can't been seen but can still be enforced, such as copyright, licenses, right-of-way, and easements.

Indemnified: An agreement to protect someone from loss or damage. Reimburse, compensate, or remunerate.

Independent Contractor: A person who works by themselves and is contracted to perform a service without being an employee for another person or company. For example, a real estate agent receives a 1099 form at the beginning of the year from his/her broker to declare on his/her taxes for the previous year.

Index Method: A statistical method. System to compute rate of return that is based on initial and terminal value. Know the original cost to build a structure without the land then multiply that by a certain number to calculate the current cost of construction.

Inflation: Increase in price, usually measured by the consumer price index.

Inheritance Tax: A tax paid by an individual who inherits property, money, and/or value. Taxes transfer to the new owner that are applied against the value of the property inherited from a deceased person.

Inspection: The act of reviewing or examining a property for diverse purposes, usually when the property is for sale before the closing or in the inspection period. Inspections can include termite, roof, and more.

Installment Contract: A type of contract in which the payments are made in installments. The buyer takes possession of the property, but the title is still in the name of the seller until the last payment is paid.

Installment Debt: Seller agrees to make an installment sale, and the buyer can make payments in a set period of time.

Instrument: A legal written document like a deed, title, lease, mortgage, or note that specifies the rights, obligations, and commitments of all the parties involved.

Interest: When a person or company purchases a property or anything else and finances it, the loan charges interest, the cost of borrowing money. The interest could be fixed or variable, and it could be calculated daily, monthly, quarterly, semiannually, or annually.

Interim Financing: Usually used for short-term loans for projects such as construction loans or buying and selling a property in a short period.

Internal Revenue Service (IRS): Revenue service for the United States federal government responsible for collecting, administering, and enforcing the tax code.

Interstate Land Sales Full Disclosure Act: Act of Congress passed in 1968 that protects consumers (buyers) from companies that fraudulently sell land. Regulates land developers and requires them to disclose everything related to or affecting the land.

Intestate: To die without having made a will.

Intrinsic Value: Intrinsic value with tangible possession. The value of an asset in the present and not for more than it is worth or the possibility of a greater or lesser value in the future.

Investment: The act or method of investing money for profit. Example: A person can expect to make a profit from an investment in a property.

Involuntary Lien: Occurs when a person or company does not pay a debt and the government or others can put a lien on the property. It becomes an involuntary levy that owners have not agreed to, such as a tax lien or judgment.

J

Jeopardy: Danger, risk. Example: to make a property the collateral in a risky transaction.

Joint Tenancy: Holding a property between two or more parties; when one dies, the property passes to the surviving joint tenant and not to the deceased heirs because the interest is undivided.

Joint Venture: A commercial enterprise started jointly between two or more parties for a specific business purpose and for a specified time without being continuous as a corporation or regular company.

Judicial Precedent: Legal case law. Precedent jurisprudence, decided by the first courts. Lower courts must follow the decisions of higher courts.

Judgment: Retribution, court order, punishment, and/or penalty.

Judgment Creditor: The party who is owed a debt, has proven they are owed the debt, and has received from the court a decree that the debtor will pay that debt.

Junior Lien: Subordinated levy, such as a second mortgage from a property used as a collateral when there is still another loan.

Junk Fee: Series of charges that the bank/lender imposes at the closing of a mortgage that could be lower. Buyer can ask the lender to lower them if the costs are too high.

Jurisdiction: The geographic area for which the government has jurisdiction: national, state, county, or city.

Just Compensation: Amount paid (usually considered fair market value) to an owner for his property when it is acquired by the government for public use. It is required to be paid by the Fifth Amendment to the U.S. Constitution when private property is taken.

K

Kickback: Fee or rebate paid to an agent in a transaction as an incentive to refer customers to a particular provider. Paying or receiving a kickback for referring a loan originator or realtor is illegal.

Kicker: Additional payment required to get a loan approved in addition to the main interest being charged.

Kiosk: Standalone booth in a mall to sell anything: newspapers, timeshares, real estate, sunglasses, etc.

L

Laches: Unreasonable delay in making a claim or assertion and not moving forward at a normal speed.

Land: Ground, the solid surface of the earth that includes trees, minerals, crops, etc.

Land Lease: Agreement to rent out the land only between the landowner and tenant.

Landlord: Owner of a property, house, building, or land; the entity rented or leased to is a tenant.

Latent Defect: A fault in a property for sale noticed in inspection before the closing that is not easily visible and is difficult to detect; the seller may not know about it.

Lease: Lease agreement between tenant and landlord for a certain time and price to rent a property.

Lease Option: Lease contract with option to purchase during or at the end of the lease. Must stipulate all conditions of the purchase agreement.

Lease Purchase: Purchase after lease, usually used for tax purposes and long term. Rent-to-own-contract. Also known as a lease purchase agreement.

Leaseback: Sale with a rental agreement afterward. Short form (sale-and-leaseback). Agreement where a person or company sells the asset then leases the property and continues to be able to use the property, but no longer owns the property.

Leasehold Estate: The tenant of a property has the exclusive right to occupy the property for a specified time. Usually requires a written lease agreement.

Legacy: Money, wealth, and/or property left by the deceased person to someone in a will.

Legal Description: A legal geographical description of a property to precisely locate the plot, parcel, and boundaries of land.

Legality of Object: A real estate contract must be entered into for a legal purpose. If the purpose of the contract is for illegal means or to commit a crime, the contract can be voided.

Legally Competent Parties: A person who is legally capable (not a minor), competent, and mentally able to enter into an agreement.

Letter of Commitment: Formal binding agreement between the lender and the buyer indicating that the borrower has been preapproved and the terms of the loan have been established.

Letter of Credit: Letter issued by a bank to another institution or bank to serve as a guarantee that the tenant will pay their commercial lease payments. Typically used in place of a security deposit in commercial real estate transactions.

Letter of Intent: Initial document negotiated between tenant and landlord or buyer and seller. Signals the intention to move forward and outlines the conditions before finalizing the actual agreement.

Letter of Opinion: Letter of opinion on the value of a house without showing evidence of other properties as would be done in a formal appraisal.

Leverage: Using other people's money for investments and expecting to make greater profits than the interest charged for the money borrowed.

Levy: A tax, fee, or fine. To seize funds or property to pay a debt.

Liability: Financial obligation, responsibility, or debt. Amount payable or future services payable.

License: Permission to work in a profession. Example: a real estate license, insurance license, etc.

Lien: Right to withhold to pay a tax or levy. An encumbrance against a property until the debt owed by the person or entity is paid or discharged.

Lien Theory: In lien theory states, the borrower holds the title to the property until the loan is paid. If the debtor does not pay the creditor, they creditor may exercise a mortgage judgment to satisfy the obligation.

Life Cycle Costing: Total cost of ownership of an asset, tracking the actual costs and revenue generated over the lifetime of the asset.

Life Estate: The ability of a person to live in a property for their remaining lifetime. They share ownership of the property with a person or persons, and the ownership reverts to them when the first individual dies.

Life Tenant: Someone who holds a property over his or her lifetime.

Limited Partnership: A form of partnership in which there is at least one general partner and another limited partner(s). The general partner has unlimited liability, whereas the limited partners' liability is limited to their investment.

Liquidated Damage: A commonly used clause in real estate to settle damages; a settlement of damages occurs if one of the parties does not comply with the contract.

Liquidity: Easy and fast way to convert assets into cash.

Lis Pendens: Notice that a lawsuit has been filed on a property; the property has pending litigation in court.

Listing Agreement: Contract/agreement between a broker/agent and the seller for a fee to sell or rent a property.

Listing Broker: Real estate broker representing the seller, also known as the seller agent.

Littoral Rights: Water coastal rights and ownership of rivers and lakes to the median high-water mark adjacent to the property.

Loan Modification: Modification of the existing loan and terms on which the bank and the debtor agree to modify. Example: the interest rate of the loan, payment schedule, etc.

Loan Origination Fee: Fee or commission that is charged to a borrower or client to originate a loan. It is commonly a percentage of the loan.

Loan Originator: Person who handles the loan processing of a borrower/buyer.

Loan-to-Value Ratio (LTV): The percentage of the loan balance to the property value. Considered the risk the lender takes to provide the loan. Formula: amount borrowed/property value = (loan to value)*100 = LTV percentage.

Loft Apartment: Originally industrial properties that became homes. Also, an open and elevated area in a room like an attic.

Lot-and-Block (recorded plat) System: Lot and block survey system is a method to identify land or lots within a subdivision. Method used in United States and Canada.

Low-Income Housing (Qualified): Homes that are eligible for a special tax credit as a dollar-to-dollar credit; low-income housing tax reform act of 1986.

M

Maintenance: Performing repairs to preserve a property over its lifetime to prevent damage.

Maintenance Fee: Payment to a condo board or homeowner association to administer, maintain, and manage the development.

Management Agreement: An agreement to administer, pay the bills of the development, and keep the properties in good condition. Also known as property management.

Marital Deduction: A type of tax law that allows a person to give assets to his/her spouse with a reduced or no tax when the asset is transferred.

Market: The sale of properties, residential and commercial. Also indicates whether it's a buyers' or sellers' market.

Market Price: Current market price at which a property could be sold or purchased.

Market Value: Highest price a buyer will pay for a property according to the market that a seller is also willing to accept in a reasonably marketable time.

Marketable of Title: A title free and clear of any reasonable doubt or litigation.

Marketing Plan: A comprehensive plan that defines the strategies to market a property for sale.

Master Plan: A zoning plan for governmental purposes. Long-term master plan to develop a town, city, rural area, and more.

Mechanic's Lien: The lien of a construction company or builder who attaches a debt to a property for non-payment of supplied labor or materials to improve the property.

Meridian: An imaginary line from north to south crossing the baseline that encircles the earth.

Metes-and-bounds Description: System or method of describing land parcel measurements and boundaries.

Mill: One thousandth; one-tenth of a penny. In real estate, $1 of property taxes assessed per $1000 in property value.

Minor: Younger than the required legal age to execute a contract.

Minority: Group of people (either by race, origin, religion, etc.), protected by law to avoid discrimination in housing and other services.

Minority Discount: Discount for being a minority; reduction of the market value of the property due to lack of marketability.

Misrepresentation: Act of giving a false statement or representation; the misrepresenting person may know or not know what they are saying is false.

Modification: Change of a clause in the contract or mortgage loan. Action of changing something.

Monetary Policy: The policy/monetary standard of the Federal Reserve bank that controls the supply of the currency.

Month-to-Month Tenancy: Month-to-month rent (period of 30 days) that can be canceled any month.

Mortgage: A legal written instrument that secures a debt and sets up payment terms in a property.

Mortgage Banker: The banker, a company that issues mortgage loans.

Mortgage Broker: Mortgage Agent (This is an older term. Now they're known as a Loan Originator.)

Mortgage Lien: Lien on a property that secures mortgage payments and debt.

Mortgage Modification: Treasury Department legislation that provides banks with incentives to prevent homeowners from losing their property. Banks give an option to modify the loan for a better loan condition. It is a change in the loan terms to reduce the interest, payments, and extend the number of months or years in the loan.

Mortgage Pool: Group of loans to be sold on the secondary market or sold in the capital market.

Mortgagee: The party that lends money such as the bank or lender.

Mortgagor: Mortgage debtor, the one who pledges a property as collateral to get a loan.

Multiperil Policy: A policy that covers different hazards and risks such as accidents, fire, civilian unrest, etc.

Multiple Listing Clause: A clause that gives permission to the broker to put the property in the MLS (Multiple Listing Service) to have more exposure for the property with other brokers who could also sell it.

Multiple Listing Service (MLS): Multiple selling service where agents and brokers agree to work and share their commissions for the same purpose.

Municipal Utility District: Provides alternate funding for developers to create infrastructure such as water, sewer, etc.

Multiplier: A factor/ratio used to multiply an important value. Example: GRM (gross rent multiplier).

N

Narrative Appraisal Report: The most detailed and extensive appraisal report, allowing appraisers to summarize and make conclusions about their findings in the property.

National Association of Realtors (NAR): Association dedicated to promoting professionalism among real estate agents in all 50 states.

Negative Amortization: Negative debt repayment. Instead of decreasing, the loan balance increases over time because the payments are not sufficient to cover the interest cost.

Negotiable Instrument: Negotiable title, promise of payment that is transferred from one individual to another.

Negotiation: Negotiations on price are typical practice in real estate contracts between buyers and sellers.

Neighborhood: Areas of similar properties that could be residential or commercial subdivisions.

Net Lease: The tenant is required to pay expenses in addition to rent, such as utilities, taxes, insurance, etc.

Net Listing: Net sales agreement. The seller has a minimum price they will accept, and the broker's commission is anything above that minimum price.

Net Operating Income (NOI): Difference between gross income and operating expenses.

Net Price: Net price of a home for sale. The seller has a minimum price they will accept, and the agent receives a commission only on the amount the buyer pays over the minimum price.

No Homogeneity: Lack of similarity among properties; no two parcels are the same.

Nonconforming Use: Noncompliant use of a property that was allowed when the zoning was established but is no longer allowed now that the zoning has changed.

Normal Wear and Tear: Normal depreciation for ordinary use throughout the years.

Note: Secured by a mortgage. A promise to pay a loan.

Notice: Legal notice to a person. There are several types of notice: notice of action, cessation, completion, default, non-responsibility, and more.

Novation: Replacing one obligation with another of similar value with the acceptance of the parties involved.

Null and Void: No effect; invalid under the law.

Nuncupative Will: A will made verbally instead of written. Witnesses must be present, and the will doesn't apply to all property. It's also not valid in all states.

O

Obligee: Person who receives an obligation from another person.

Obligor: Person who gives one obligation to another. Also known as a debtor who owes money to another person or financial institution.

Obsolescence: Loss of the value of a property by outdated or depreciated feature whether structure, construction, etc.

Occupancy: Possession. Also used to determine the occupancy rate of a building.

Occupancy Permit: Permit issued by housing authorities that allows people to inhabit a property.

Offer and Acceptance: Seller accepts the buyer's offer on their property by signing the Purchase and Sale Agreement signed by the buyer.

Offeree: Recipient of the offer.

Offeror: Bidder. Person who makes the offer.

Office of Thrift Supervision (OTS): Federal institution that regulates the national savings and loan industry.

Open-end Loan: A loan that can continue to be extended by the borrower with a maximum cap on principal with the same mortgage.

Open House: House that is for sale and open for public viewing to be shown by an agent.

Open Listing: Open Sales Agreement; Non-exclusive agreement, may be sold by another agent or seller. The commission is paid only to the agent who brings the buyer. If the seller sells his/her property, there will be no commission to any agent.

Operating Expense Ratio: Percentage of operating expenses; operating expenses divided by potential gross income.

Opinion of Title: Title certificate, valid for a title. Legal opinion that attests the validity of title.

Option: The right to buy or rent a property with specific terms and within a specific time frame.

Option Listing: Agreement the seller makes (with a buyer, agent, or broker) with an option to buy the property at a specific price within a specific time frame.

Ostensible Agency: Representation that is apparent based on acts taken and not based on a written agreement.

Ownership: Property, domain. Right to the use, enjoyment of the property.

Ownership Form: Method of owning the property; example: community property, corporation, common tenure, etc.

P

Package Loan: Loan that includes the property and some personal property such as curtains, furniture, etc.

Panic Peddling: Profiting through panic, panic trafficking, is illegal. When an agent engages in panic peddling, they are recommending homeowners sell their home and leave a neighborhood when the racial composition of the neighborhood begins to change.

Parcel: Plot, piece of land in a subdivision.

Parol Evidence Rule: Rule on the admissibility of written evidence made after oral evidence, replacing the oral evidence if it contradicts.

Partition: Splitting a property among two or more people with an undivided interest.

Partnership: Association of two or more persons for profit and to achieve a shared goal.

Party Wall: Dividing wall between two units.

Passive Income: Creating income without having to be actively involved such as rents, dividends, sales, interest earned, etc.

Patent: Concession or franchise. Transfer of land by the government in perpetuity. Protection of intellectual property.

Payment Cap: Limit on how high mortgage payments can be. Maximum payment amount that can be charged to the buyer.

Percentage Lease: Lease that includes a percentage due to the landlord based on gross sales above the scheduled rent; this type of lease is commercial.

Permit: Permission issued by the government for a specific use or action.

Personal Assistant: Could be unlicensed or licensed personal assistant. Performs jobs for an agent or broker but cannot negotiate or talk about a property (if not licensed). If a licensed personal assistant, they could negotiate or talk about a property.

Personal Property: Movable property. Property that is not designated as real estate property.

Physical Deterioration: Normal or natural wear and tear caused by any means, such as hurricanes decreasing the value of the property.

Planned Unit Development (PUD): Planned development of units within an area to be used in various ways such as parks, housing, commercial developments, etc.

Planning Commission: Government commission for planning and development or conservation.

Plat Map: Map of a cadastral plan; subdivision plan, map that indicates the location of each property.

Plottage: Merging two or more adjacent plots into one to increase the value of the property.

Point of Beginning (POB): Starting point for cadastral surveying, usually a well-known landmark.

Points: Fee a buyer can pay to lower the interest rate of the loan; a percentage equivalent to 1% percent of the loan amount.

Police Power: Government power to enforce laws for the protection, health, and benefit of its citizens.

Policy: Insurance policy.

Power of Attorney: A letter that gives an individual the ability to act for another within certain limitations.

Pre-approval: Made though a bank or loan institution to an individual for the purpose of buying a property or refinancing. The letter has the amount that the buyer is pre-approved to borrow.

Pre-closing: A closing test, prepared when the actual closing is expected to be complicated.

Pre-foreclosure Sale: The sale of a property to a third party while the property is in default and before the bank repossesses the property.

Pre-sale: Sale of a house before it is built and finished.

Prepaid Items: Items the seller prepaid that are refunded by the buyer on the day of closing such as insurance, taxes, etc.

Prepayment Penalty: Fine for prepayment of a home loan.

Primary Mortgage Market: Market that serves buyers directly such as consumer banks, institutions, loan officers, mortgage brokers, etc.

Prime Rate: Most favorable interest rate offered to preferred customers.

Principal: Capital, the amount of the original loan.

Principal Broker: Broker in charge of a real estate office.

Principal, Interest, Tax, and Insurance (PITI): Included in the monthly payment to amortize the principal and pay interest as well as apply to the escrow held for taxes and insurance.

Principal Meridian: Main meridian, an imaginary line running from north to south, see *meridian*.

Prior Appropriation: Priority appropriation of water, the use of water on land by government permits.

Priority: Order for which entity will be paid based on time or location whether for unpaid taxes, liens, etc.

Private Mortgage Insurance (PMI): Private insurance against a lender's loss in the event of a default on the loan used for conventional loans when a buyer finances more than 80% loan to value. Mortgage Insurance Premium (MIP) is like PMI but is used on FHA loans.

Probate: Validation of a will through a state's legal process to see who inherits the assets.

Procuring Cause: The agent who has the right to the commission. When there are two agents involved, one is the procuring cause of the real estate transaction (the reason the sale happened).

Progression: In a subdivision, when the value of less expensive properties go up based on the value of more expensive properties in the subdivision.

Promissory Note: A promise and method of payment of a debt that is in turn transferable to a third party.

Property Management: Property manager of building complexes for maintenance, collection of rent, and other services.

Property Reports: Data on the property that will be sold or marketed.

Proprietary Lease: Lease by an owner in a coop, no service rendered from any agent.

Prorations: Credits between the buyer and seller on the day of closing, such as prepaid taxes or insurance, rent paid by tenants to the seller or buyer, taxes, and/or association fees.

Prospect: An individual who is likely to become a future customer.

Protected Class: Class/group protected by Housing and Urban Development (HUD) against discrimination in housing, a minority group.

Puffing: Exaggerated reviews and opinions.

Pur Autre Vie: For the duration of third person's life (not the beneficiary's life).

Purchase Contract: Contract/Sales Agreement between a buyer and a seller.

Pyramiding: Pyramid process; refinancing existing properties to invest that money in more properties.

Q

Quadrangle: Quadrilateral; four-sided square area of 24 miles, each quadrilateral has 16 municipalities.

Qualified: Individual who is qualified or approved for the purchase of a property.

Quantity Survey Method: Method of surveying land to evaluate all the costs of construction such as materials, equipment, labor, profit, etc.

Quiet Enjoyment: Enjoy the property without interference.

Quiet Title: A lawsuit filed to establish full title without obstacles, ready to be sold or transferred, free of encumbrances.

Quitclaim Deed: The transfer of ownership, adding or removing someone from the title.

R

Radon Gas: Radioactive gas that is harmful to health that comes from the natural breakdown of uranium.

Range: Land measuring 6 miles wide extended from north to south and measured from east to west. Also, the comparison of one price to another, such as a house valued between $100,000-$125,000.

Rate Cap: Cap on how high an interest rate can be for the life of the loan.

Ratification: Individual who agrees with the actions of another after the actions have taken place. Affirming a previously performed act.

Ready, Willing, and Able Buyer: Buyer ready, willing, and able to purchase a property under the conditions imposed and ready to start financing or buying in cash.

Real Estate Commission (In Florida, FREC): An agency that enforces real estate laws to protect the consumer and regulates agents and brokers.

Real Estate Investment Syndicate: When investors pool their resources to purchase a large property together.

Real Estate Investment Trust (REIT): A company that makes investments in real estate and allows investors to buy shares in the company.

Real Estate License Law: Real estate laws that protect consumers from fraud.

Real Estate Market: Market for buyers and sellers related to all types of real estate such as condominiums, land, houses, etc.

Real Estate Mortgage Investment Conduit (REMIC): An entity that issues multiple classes of investor interest securities backed by a mortgage portfolio.

Real Estate Recovery Fund: Fund that pays individuals who were victims of an agent to compensate for their loss.

Real Estate Settlement Procedures Act (RESPA): A law that establishes how lenders should disclose information to clients who are borrowing money for properties to help them compare terms and costs among lenders.

Real Property: Land, from below the surface into space, including everything on it. Example: trees, buildings, houses, fixtures, etc.

Realist: Database of property information used by multiple listing services.

RealQuest: Database providing information like Realist.

Realtor®: A designation given by the Board of Realtors® and the National Association of Realtors® for agents and brokers.

Realty: Just like real estate: real property, land, and buildings.

Reconciliation: All brokers holding a trust-escrow account must reconcile every month, as well as title companies and lawyers. There can be no more nor less than is allowed in the account, nor can it be mixed with other accounts.

Reconveyance Deed: Real estate transfer writing that transfers ownership from the lender to the borrower after the mortgage is paid in full.

Recording: Registration of a property in county records. Filling documents to give notice to future purchasers.

Recovery Account: Recovery account for victims of fraud or misrepresentation which could not be collected after a judgment.

Rectangular (Government) Survey System: Government rectangular terrain survey system formed by major meridians and baselines.

Redemption: The owner may network to recover his property for some form of non-compliance.

Redemption Period: The timeframe an owner is allowed to recover his property after having it repossessed in a mortgage judgment or another legal proceeding.

Redlining: The illegal practice of a loan institution denying or limiting loans in a specific community usually due to racial or ethnic discrimination.

Reduction Certificate (payoff statement): A settlement statement that specifies the amount to pay off a debt in its entirety. This certificate is issued when there is a sale, refinancing, or the owner wants to repay the loan in full.

Refinance: Replacing an older loan with a new one to lower interest, monthly payments, or take money out of the property.

Regression: Regression occurs when the largest and most valuable property is affected by the lower value of other properties in a community.

Regulation "Z": A law to clarify what and how much the costs of a loan will be to the borrower.

Rehabilitate: Rehabilitate/Restructure a property that was not habitable; improve the property.

Release Deed: Transfers ownership when the mortgage has been paid.

Remainder Interest: Residual interest passed on to a different person after their fixed interest expires. Example: interest is given to one person, then when they die, the interest passes to another.

Remodel: Change the structure or functionality of an area in a property.

Renovate: Repairs and updates to a home without changing the area's purpose.

Rent: A lease. Landlord gives the right to a tenant to use his/her property in exchange for money or other consideration. Could be short- or long-term rent.

Rent Schedule: The rental program, rental plan, or rental proposal of a property.

REO-Real Estate Owned: Properties that the bank or government agency owns and didn't sell at auction.

Repairs: Fixing a home and whatever is inside.

Replacement Cost: How much it would cost in today's market to construct a property under current conditions.

Repo: Repossess a property; foreclosure.

Repossession: Losing a mortgage judgment; the lender takes ownership of a property when loan payments are not made; recovery of the property by the landlord or owner of the rented or leased property.

Reproduction Cost: Cost to reproduce any property or furniture.

Rescission: The timeframe in which a customer can cancel a contract.

Residential Property: Property or land designated for people to live in. Example: single family homes, condos, coops, etc.

Resolution: The decision among all parties in a dispute to come to a common agreement.

Resolution Trust Corporation (RTC): A corporation created by FIRREA to liquidate the assets of failed savings and loan institutions.

Restrictive Covenants: An agreement made between two parties that limits how the property can be used.

Reverse Annuity Mortgage (RAM): For people over 62 years old. Borrowers make no payments toward the principal and interest and the debt increases over time.

Reversionary Interest: Future interest in a property held by one party after transferring ownership to another party.

Reversionary Right: Right of reversal to a landlord to occupy or continue to occupy the property, even if the lease has expired.

Revocation: To revoke an agent's license. They can never practice as an agent; for example, if FREC takes away a license it is usually indefinite.

Right of Appropriation: Right of the government to appropriate or change the function of a property. Example: changing the course of a river for a specific purpose.

Right of Entry: Right to access the property of another without committing trespass. Can also mean taking or retaking a property.

Right-of-way: Right of passage through another person's property.

Riparian Rights: Riverside rights; access to the water abutting a property whether lake, river, etc.

Risk Management: Limiting the risks inherent in real estate; could mitigate risk by purchasing insurance or following best practices for certain activities.

Robo-signer: Lawyers or bank employees who sign foreclosure documents without reviewing them. Investigating the validity of the information is required by law.

Rules and Regulations: Set of guidelines that protect the public, industry, profession, and more.

Rural: Area outside or away from the city such as ranches or farms.

S

"S" Corporation: A small corporation. Has tax benefits (the corporation does not pay taxes); losses and profits are distributed between the owners/shareholders.

Safe Rate: Interest rate on low-risk investments.

Sale and Leaseback: Sale to a buyer followed by a lease from the buyer.

Sale Pending: A property that is awaiting settlement or is in the final stages of escrow and has not yet closed.

Sales Comparison Approach: Estimated value of a property based on past sales price among other comparable properties.

Sales Contract: Contract for sale and purchase agreement between a buyer and a seller who agree to the terms.

Sales Price: Amount/sum/price agreed to in an agreement/contract to buy/sell a property.

Salesperson: Real estate agent and/or broker who practices real estate.

Satisfaction of Mortgage: A document showing a mortgage is paid in full.

Second Home: A property maintained by an individual to spend part of the year in or visit regularly.

Secondary Market: The market where banks and investors resell the loans they obtained in the primary market.

Section: One square mile of land containing 640 acres; there are 36 sections in a township-district.

Section 8 Housing: Program to help low-income individuals obtain rental assistance.

Security: Property that serves as collateral for a debt.

Security Deposit: Money set aside by the buyer to show a serious interest in buying a property and executing an agreement.

Seller Finance: The owner is financing the sale of the property.

Seller's Market: Market in favor of the seller. Occurs when there is a lower inventory of properties.

Separate Property: Separate ownership of property by a spouse; may have been obtained prior to marriage, received as an inheritance or gift, or purchased with funds that do not belong to the partner.

Servient Tenement: If there is a dominant tenement (estate), the servient tenement may be required to allow the dominant tenement right-of-way access to the property.

Setback: Builders are required to leave some distance between the property line and where they build.

Severalty: Possession of a property by a single owner.

Severance: Physical separation of an item that was attached to a property. Changes an item from real property to personal property.

Sharecropping: Share the agricultural crop or profit between the tenant and the landlord as part of a lease agreement.

Sheriff's Deed: At a sheriff's sale, the deed given to the purchaser. A property is sold at a sheriff's sale to pay the judgment against the owner.

Shopping Center: A mall, a collection of small and large department stores and restaurants that share parking and more.

Short Sale: Bank and buyer agree to sell the property to another buyer for less than the loan amount.

Sinking Fund: Amortization fund on an account earning interest that is kept aside for future repairs.

Special Agent: A trained agent who knows how to search for a buyer who is ready, willing, and able to buy the property that an owner gives him to sell. The ability of an agent to work on a specific property for a specific purpose to benefit his/her client.

Special Assessment: A tax used for improvements, a special benefit or use such as a street.

Special Warranty Deed: The seller guarantees anything that happened only during the time of their ownership.

Specific Lien: Lien, loan secured by a specific property.

Specific Performance: Court order that forces the parties to comply with the terms of the agreement. Assumes that monetary compensation does not adequately cover the loss.

Spot Zoning: Zone planning, change of zoning for a small area. Example: change from residential to commercial in a subdivision; is not generally allowed in the courts.

Square-foot Method: Method for calculating value per square foot.

Statute of Frauds: A law that says certain contracts must be in writing to be valid and prevent fraud.

Statute of Limitations: Prescription act, limits the time an individual has to bring a lawsuit.

Statutory Lien: Involuntary lien imposed on a property like a tax lien if property taxes are not paid.

Statutory Redemption: A debtor's right for a specific time to recover their property after it has been sold in foreclosure by paying specified fees and payments.

Steering: Discriminating against a minority group by not showing them properties in certain areas.

Straight-Line Method of Depreciation: A linear and uniform method that calculates depreciation for tax purposes for the life of the property.

Straight/Term Loan: Linear loan/term where only interest is paid, and the entire principal remains until the end of the loan term.

Subagent: An agent who works with another broker, working together to make a joint transaction. Example: the listing agent and buyer's agent are subagents.

Subdivider: The person who buys a piece of land and divides it up into smaller lots to put them up for sale and make more profits.

Subdivision: Divide land into lots/parcels.

Subdivision and Development Ordinances: Rules for subdivisions, development, and urbanization to establish building requirements.

Sublease: Initial tenant rents to a third party with the authorization of the landlord; either the entire space or part of it.

Subletting: The initial renter rents the space to a third party for the remaining term of the rental agreement; must have permission from the landlord or be allowed in the contract.

Subordination: Move to a lower priority. Example: a loan goes from being a first mortgage to being a second mortgage.

Subordination Agreement: Contract that reorders debt, prioritizing some loans over others. Subject to the agreement of all parties.

Subrogation: Replacing one creditor with another to make sure the lender recovers the money in case the person dies or does not pay.

Substitution: In an appraisal, setting a price for replacement or obtaining the item.

Subsurface Rights: Land and underground rights.

Supply: Availability of properties for sale.

Supply and Demand: Real estate available to buy and sell and the price based on this principle.

Suit for Possession: A petition for possession by the landlord who legally owns the property to remove a tenant either for breach of the lease or when the agreement is terminated.

Suit to Quiet Title: Petition to get full title.

Surety Bond: Warranty used in certain areas that is required to practice or open a business such as title companies, banks.

Surface Rights: Rights to use and do whatever you want on the surface of the terrain within the zoning rules.

Survey: Measure of a property in both land and construction by a licensed surveyor.

Survivorship: The one who is a survivor on a property in common with another person.

Syndicate: Group of investors who sells its investments in stocks or units and raises profits to continue investing.

T

Tacking: Merger of two mortgages; the joining of two periods of possession.

Tangible Property: Physical property such as furniture; property that is touchable and can be seen.

Tax Basis: The initial investment in a property used to measure remaining depreciation and future gain.

Tax Credit: Credit that directly reduces income tax due that would otherwise be paid.

Tax Deductible: A reduction in gross income that creates a reduction in taxes payable.

Tax Deed: When the previous owner fails to pay taxes on a property, the deed is granted to the government and can then be sold at auction.

Tax Foreclosure: Judgment for non-payment of taxes; if the owner does not pay their property taxes, they lose ownership of the property.

Tax Lien: A lien recorded on the property for non-payment of property taxes.

Tax Rate: A percentage/ratio of the tax paid.

Tax Roll: List of all taxable properties in the county and other jurisdictions.

Tax Sale: Tax auction, sale of a property for not paying taxes.

Taxation: A method the government uses to collect money; used to pay for government operations.

Tenancy by the Entirety: Joint possession between married couples; each possesses 100% of the property. If one dies, it passes to the survivor.

Tenancy in Common: Co-ownership of a property, tenure in common. Undivided with no right of survivorship.

Tenancy in Partnership: Co-ownership with two or more people. Partners cannot transfer their ownership outside the partnership.

Tenant: Occupant of a property; tenant has the right of possession for the time of the lease.

Tenant Improvements: Improvements made by the tenant usually within the home.

Termite Inspection: Inspection by a qualified inspector to assess termite damage or infestation of the property.

Testament: Will to dispose of a person's property after their death.

Testate: A valid will exists at the time of death.

Testator: A person who makes a valid will before they die.

Tier (township strip): Bands or lines in the municipal district 6 square miles wide.

Time Is of the Essence: Clause used in real estate contracts to determine the amount of time to perform obligations in the contract.

Timeshare: Share of a vacation property among several owners entitled to possession for a specific timeframe.

Title: Legal instrument that shows evidence of property/land ownership.

Title Insurance: Insurance against title defects; guarantees an owner's rights so that no other person can claim the property.

Title Report: Report which describes the legal status of a property and documents title research.

Title Search: Investigation of a title in the public record to confirm the legal owner.

Title Theory: In some states, the title is given to the borrower until the debt is paid or canceled; otherwise, it is in the name and possession of the lender.

Torrens System: System that is used in some states to register titles.

Township: District/Municipal Division; municipality with 36 square miles with 6 miles on each side.

Trade Fixture: Furniture attached to a property. Example: a commercial business installs shelves in their offices.

Transfer Tax: Tax to transfer property from one owner to another.

Trulia: Supplier of statistics on real estate data, prices, and market activity. Real estate search engine.

Trust: A legal arrangement that holds assets for an eventual beneficiary.

Trust Account: Escrow account. A separate account from a real estate broker's operating account where a broker deposits client escrow deposit money. The maximum amount a broker can deposit of their own money to maintain the broker account is $1,000.00; for a property management company, their maximum is $5,000.00.

Trust Deed: Deed that the lender uses as collateral. In some states, the borrower transfers the deed to the lender until the property is paid in full.

Trust Deed Lien: Trust deed levy; a lien on a property.

Trustee: A person in charge of managing another's property with their legal authorization.

Trustee's Deed: Like Deed of Trust or Deed Trust, an instrument used to protect the lender in the case of default.

Trustor: Trust creator; in real estate, the borrower.

Truth-in-Lending Act (TILA): Law that regulates the cost of loans. See Regulation "Z."

Turnkey Project: The builder/developer gives the keys to the buyer or lessee after the development or improvement is complete.

U

Underimprovement: Improvements made that are below the standard.

Underwriter: An employee of the lender who carefully reviews the loan and verifies that everything is correct before approving the loan.

Unenforceable Contract: Contract that cannot be enforced by the courts. Agreement without consideration or obligation.

Uniform Commercial Code: Statement of funding terms; group of standardized state laws in the commercial area.

Unilateral Contract: Only one party is obliged or contingent to the agreement.

Unit: An apartment, office, or studio.

Unit-in-place Method: Itemized costs to replace a building, from construction, installation, and more.

Unit of Ownership: Basic property unit; share.

Universal Agent: Universal representation that a principal gives to his agent; the power to act on his/her behalf to represent him/her with full power.

Urban Property: City or town.

Useful Life: The number of years a building, house, or property can be expected to be used before its value is fully depreciated.

Usury: Charge a higher interest than legal in the area or state.

Utilities: Services such as water, electricity, etc., which are required to occupy the property.

V

VA Loan: Loan backed by the U.S. Department of Veterans Affairs. Individuals and their spouses who have retired or served a certain time in the military can purchase a home at 100% financing.

Vacancy Rate: Percentage of units in a building that are not occupied versus occupied.

Vacant Land: Unused, empty land.

Valid Contract: A legally binding real estate contract.

Value: Something of value. Value of all rights derived from one property; amount of one thing to be given in exchange for another.

Variance: Permission for a variation in zoning by creating an exception.

Vendee: Buyer/purchaser within the requirements of an agreement.

Vendor: Seller who owns a property for sale within a contract.

Venture Capital: Money raised to fund newer businesses; they carry higher investment risks.

Violation: Act or condition contrary to the law.

Void: Null; has no legal force or effect.

Void Contract: Null contract; has no effect as it does not have what is necessary to be valid.

Voidable: Able to be rescinded by either party, but only by taking a specific action and not by itself.

Voidable Contract: A contract that can be voided by either party.

Voluntary Lien: Lien on a property with the authorization of the owner of the property such as a mortgage.

W

Waiver: Voluntarily give up or postpone a claim.

Walk-through Inspection: Inspection that is done before signing a purchase or rental agreement.

Warranty: Promise within a contract.

Waste: Misuse and abuse of a property that can negatively affect the value of the property.

Will: Legal document to transfer goods or property to a beneficiary.

Workers Compensation Acts: Insurance requirement for employers to compensate employees in case of an accident at work.

Wraparound Loan: A contingent/subordinated loan (usually offered by the seller) that is wrapped around an original primary loan; refinancing that envelops several loans without changing the order of the first mortgage.

Writ of Execution: Commandment of execution issued by court order that sends a sheriff to obtain assets as monetary satisfaction.

Writ of Possession: Court order for possession of a property; evict a tenant from a property.

Write-Down: Decreased value of a property due to a change in its market price. Accounting term related to a property's book value.

Wrongful Foreclosure: Mortgage lawsuit conducted illegally or incorrectly, in which the owner may sue to recover his property.

Y

Yard: Land either to the front, back, or side of a property. The land between the property line and a structure built on it.

Yield: Profit from an investment or loan.

Yield to Maturity (YTM): Annual rate of return on an investment.

Z

Zero Lot Line: Building close to or abutting a wall or the property line separating one property from another.

Zillow: Popular internet site offering property information for sale or rent, showing comparable properties and offering a client lead generator.

Zip skinny: Source of demographic information organized by area code.

Zone: Areas of the county and/or city governed by zoning.

Zoning Map: Map of an area; urban plan indicating current development designations.

Zoning Ordinance: How property in a city or county can be developed or used.

Chapter 7

Success Action Planner

Bonus gifts for you.

The Success Action Planner. I recommend you use this tool for a minimum of 90 days. The Planner includes:

1. A three-month undated planner calendar to take immediate action
2. A 15-week undated planner
3. An operation plan
4. An action plan
5. A monthly log of calls: realized goals, what you learned, and results
6. Notes
7. Vision board (four different types of models)
8. To do list
9. A place to note the most important chapters and pages you want to remember from this book
10. Business debut timetable (blank)
11. A customer form for your business debut

Month: _____

Monday	Tuesday	Wednesday	Thursday	Friday
☐	☐	☐	☐	☐
☐	☐	☐	☐	☐
☐	☐	☐	☐	☐
☐	☐	☐	☐	☐
☐	☐	☐	☐	☐

Number of Monthly Goals Reached:

_____Social Media Posts _____Handed Out Business Cards _____New Contracts

_____Calls _____Appointments _____Purchases

_____Talked to People _____Listing Presentations _____Rentals

_____New Contacts _____Listings _____Referrals

20_____

Saturday	Sunday
☐	☐
☐	☐
☐	☐
☐	☐
☐	☐

Monthly Affirmation: _____

_____

_____

_____

Monthly Goals

☐ _____
☐ _____
☐ _____
☐ _____
☐ _____
☐ _____

Monthly To-Do List

☐ _____
☐ _____
☐ _____
☐ _____
☐ _____
☐ _____
☐ _____
☐ _____
☐ _____
☐ _____

NOTES:

_____

_____

_____

_____

_____

_____

Week of:_____

Priorities	Monday ____	Tuesday ____	Wednesday ____	Thursday ____
	☐	☐	☐	☐
	☐	☐	☐	☐
	☐	☐	☐	☐
	☐	☐	☐	☐
	☐	☐	☐	☐
	☐	☐	☐	☐
8				
9				
10				
11				
12				
1				
2				
3				
4				
5				
6				
7				

Number of Weekly Goals Reached:

_____Social Media Posts	_____Handed Out Business Cards	_____New Contracts
_____Calls	_____Appointments	_____Purchases
_____Talked to People	_____Listing Presentations	_____Rentals
_____New Contacts	_____Listings	_____Referrals

Month: _____

Friday _____	Saturday _____	Sunday _____
☐	☐	☐
☐	☐	☐
☐	☐	☐
☐	☐	☐
☐	☐	☐
☐	☐	☐
8		
9		
10		
11		
12		
1		
2		
3		
4		
5		
6		
7		

Weekly Goals

☐ _____
☐ _____
☐ _____
☐ _____
☐ _____
☐ _____
☐ _____

Weekly To-Do List

☐ _____
☐ _____
☐ _____
☐ _____
☐ _____
☐ _____
☐ _____
☐ _____
☐ _____
☐ _____

NOTES:

_____
_____
_____

Weekly Affirmation: _____

_____
_____
_____
_____

Week of:_____

Monday _____	Tuesday _____	Wednesday _____	Thursday _____
☐	☐	☐	☐
☐	☐	☐	☐
☐	☐	☐	☐
☐	☐	☐	☐
☐	☐	☐	☐
☐	☐	☐	☐
8			
9			
10			
11			
12			
1			
2			
3			
4			
5			
6			
7			

Priorities

Number of Weekly Goals Reached:

_____Social Media Posts	_____Handed Out Business Cards	_____New Contracts
_____Calls	_____Appointments	_____Purchases
_____Talked to People	_____Listing Presentations	_____Rentals
_____New Contacts	_____Listings	_____Referrals

Month: _____

Friday _____	Saturday _____	Sunday _____
☐	☐	☐
☐	☐	☐
☐	☐	☐
☐	☐	☐
☐	☐	☐
☐	☐	☐
8		
9		
10		
11		
12		
1		
2		
3		
4		
5		
6		
7		

Weekly Goals

☐ _____
☐ _____
☐ _____
☐ _____
☐ _____
☐ _____
☐ _____

Weekly To-Do List

☐ _____
☐ _____
☐ _____
☐ _____
☐ _____
☐ _____
☐ _____
☐ _____
☐ _____
☐ _____

NOTES:

_____
_____
_____
_____
_____
_____

Weekly Affirmation: _____

_____
_____
_____
_____

Week of:_____

Priorities	Monday _____	Tuesday _____	Wednesday _____	Thursday _____
	☐	☐	☐	☐
	☐	☐	☐	☐
	☐	☐	☐	☐
	☐	☐	☐	☐
	☐	☐	☐	☐
	☐	☐	☐	☐
8				
9				
10				
11				
12				
1				
2				
3				
4				
5				
6				
7				

Number of Weekly Goals Reached:

_____Social Media Posts	_____Handed Out Business Cards	_____New Contracts
_____Calls	_____Appointments	_____Purchases
_____Talked to People	_____Listing Presentations	_____Rentals
_____New Contacts	_____Listings	_____Referrals

Month: _____

Friday _____	Saturday _____	Sunday _____
☐	☐	☐
☐	☐	☐
☐	☐	☐
☐	☐	☐
☐	☐	☐
☐	☐	☐
8		
9		
10		
11		
12		
1		
2		
3		
4		
5		
6		
7		

Weekly Goals

☐ _____
☐ _____
☐ _____
☐ _____
☐ _____
☐ _____
☐ _____

Weekly To-Do List

☐ _____
☐ _____
☐ _____
☐ _____
☐ _____
☐ _____
☐ _____
☐ _____
☐ _____
☐ _____

NOTES:

_____
_____
_____
_____

Weekly Affirmation: _____

_____
_____
_____
_____
_____

Week of:_____

Priorities	Monday _____	Tuesday _____	Wednesday _____	Thursday _____
	☐	☐	☐	☐
	☐	☐	☐	☐
	☐	☐	☐	☐
	☐	☐	☐	☐
	☐	☐	☐	☐
	☐	☐	☐	☐
8				
9				
10				
11				
12				
1				
2				
3				
4				
5				
6				
7				

Number of Weekly Goals Reached:

_____Social Media Posts _____Handed Out Business Cards _____New Contracts

_____Calls _____Appointments _____Purchases

_____Talked to People _____Listing Presentations _____Rentals

_____New Contacts _____Listings _____Referrals

Month: _____

Weekly Goals

Friday _____	Saturday _____	Sunday _____
☐	☐	☐
☐	☐	☐
☐	☐	☐
☐	☐	☐
☐	☐	☐
☐	☐	☐
8		
9		
10		
11		
12		
1		
2		
3		
4		
5		
6		
7		

☐ _____
☐ _____
☐ _____
☐ _____
☐ _____
☐ _____
☐ _____

Weekly To-Do List

☐ _____
☐ _____
☐ _____
☐ _____
☐ _____
☐ _____
☐ _____
☐ _____
☐ _____
☐ _____

NOTES:

_____
_____
_____
_____
_____
_____

Weekly Affirmation: _____

Week of:_____

	Monday _____	Tuesday _____	Wednesday _____	Thursday _____
Priorities	☐	☐	☐	☐
	☐	☐	☐	☐
	☐	☐	☐	☐
	☐	☐	☐	☐
	☐	☐	☐	☐
	☐	☐	☐	☐
	8			
	9			
	10			
	11			
	12			
	1			
	2			
	3			
	4			
	5			
	6			
	7			

Number of Weekly Goals Reached:

_____Social Media Posts	_____Handed Out Business Cards	_____New Contracts
_____Calls	_____Appointments	_____Purchases
_____Talked to People	_____Listing Presentations	_____Rentals
_____New Contacts	_____Listings	_____Referrals

Month: _____

Friday _____	Saturday _____	Sunday _____
☐	☐	☐
☐	☐	☐
☐	☐	☐
☐	☐	☐
☐	☐	☐
☐	☐	☐
8		
9		
10		
11		
12		
1		
2		
3		
4		
5		
6		
7		

Weekly Goals

☐ _____
☐ _____
☐ _____
☐ _____
☐ _____
☐ _____
☐ _____

Weekly To-Do List

☐ _____
☐ _____
☐ _____
☐ _____
☐ _____
☐ _____
☐ _____
☐ _____
☐ _____
☐ _____

NOTES:

_____
_____
_____
_____
_____
_____
_____

Weekly Affirmation: _____

_____
_____
_____
_____

Approaches/Posts/Calls Goal Tracking

Start 1	2	3	4	5
6	7	8	9	10
11	12	13	14	15
16	17	18	19	20
21	22	23	24	25
26	27	28	29	30
31	32	33	34	35
36	37	38	39	40
41	42	43	44	45
Goal 46	47	48	49	50

Monthly Realized Goals

☐ _____
☐ _____
☐ _____
☐ _____
☐ _____
☐ _____
☐ _____
☐ _____
☐ _____

What did you learn this month?

_____

_____

_____

_____

_____

_____

Results:

_____

_____

_____

Notes:

Month: _____

Monday	Tuesday	Wednesday	Thursday	Friday
☐	☐	☐	☐	☐
☐	☐	☐	☐	☐
☐	☐	☐	☐	☐
☐	☐	☐	☐	☐
☐	☐	☐	☐	☐

Number of Monthly Goals Reached:

_____Social Media Posts   _____Handed Out Business Cards   _____New Contracts

_____Calls   _____Appointments   _____Purchases

_____Talked to People   _____Listing Presentations   _____Rentals

_____New Contacts   _____Listings   _____Referrals

20_____

Saturday	Sunday
☐	☐
☐	☐
☐	☐
☐	☐
☐	☐

Monthly Affirmation: _____
_____
_____
_____

Monthly Goals

☐ _____
☐ _____
☐ _____
☐ _____
☐ _____
☐ _____

Monthly To-Do List

☐ _____
☐ _____
☐ _____
☐ _____
☐ _____
☐ _____
☐ _____
☐ _____
☐ _____
☐ _____

NOTES:

_____
_____
_____
_____
_____
_____

Week of:_____

Priorities	Monday _____	Tuesday _____	Wednesday _____	Thursday _____
	☐	☐	☐	☐
	☐	☐	☐	☐
	☐	☐	☐	☐
	☐	☐	☐	☐
	☐	☐	☐	☐
	☐	☐	☐	☐
8				
9				
10				
11				
12				
1				
2				
3				
4				
5				
6				
7				

Number of Weekly Goals Reached:

_____Social Media Posts   _____Handed Out Business Cards   _____New Contracts

_____Calls   _____Appointments   _____Purchases

_____Talked to People   _____Listing Presentations   _____Rentals

_____New Contacts   _____Listings   _____Referrals

Month: _____

Friday _____	Saturday _____	Sunday _____
☐	☐	☐
☐	☐	☐
☐	☐	☐
☐	☐	☐
☐	☐	☐
☐	☐	☐
8		
9		
10		
11		
12		
1		
2		
3		
4		
5		
6		
7		

Weekly Goals

☐ _____
☐ _____
☐ _____
☐ _____
☐ _____
☐ _____
☐ _____

Weekly To-Do List

☐ _____
☐ _____
☐ _____
☐ _____
☐ _____
☐ _____
☐ _____
☐ _____
☐ _____
☐ _____

NOTES:

_____
_____
_____
_____
_____
_____

Weekly Affirmation: _____

_____
_____
_____
_____

Week of:_____

Priorities	Monday _____	Tuesday _____	Wednesday _____	Thursday _____
	☐	☐	☐	☐
	☐	☐	☐	☐
	☐	☐	☐	☐
	☐	☐	☐	☐
	☐	☐	☐	☐
	☐	☐	☐	☐
8				
9				
10				
11				
12				
1				
2				
3				
4				
5				
6				
7				

Number of Weekly Goals Reached:

_____Social Media Posts   _____Handed Out Business Cards   _____New Contracts

_____Calls   _____Appointments   _____Purchases

_____Talked to People   _____Listing Presentations   _____Rentals

_____New Contacts   _____Listings   _____Referrals

Month: _____

Weekly Goals

Friday _____	Saturday _____	Sunday _____
☐	☐	☐
☐	☐	☐
☐	☐	☐
☐	☐	☐
☐	☐	☐
☐	☐	☐
8		
9		
10		
11		
12		
1		
2		
3		
4		
5		
6		
7		

Weekly Goals
☐ _____
☐ _____
☐ _____
☐ _____
☐ _____
☐ _____
☐ _____

Weekly To-Do List
☐ _____
☐ _____
☐ _____
☐ _____
☐ _____
☐ _____
☐ _____
☐ _____
☐ _____
☐ _____

NOTES:
_____
_____
_____

Weekly Affirmation: _____
_____
_____
_____
_____

Week of:_____

Priorities	Monday _____	Tuesday _____	Wednesday _____	Thursday _____
	☐	☐	☐	☐
	☐	☐	☐	☐
	☐	☐	☐	☐
	☐	☐	☐	☐
	☐	☐	☐	☐
	☐	☐	☐	☐
	8			
	9			
	10			
	11			
	12			
	1			
	2			
	3			
	4			
	5			
	6			
	7			

Number of Weekly Goals Reached:

_____Social Media Posts   _____Handed Out Business Cards   _____New Contracts

_____Calls   _____Appointments   _____Purchases

_____Talked to People   _____Listing Presentations   _____Rentals

_____New Contacts   _____Listings   _____Referrals

Month: _____

Weekly Goals

Friday _____	Saturday _____	Sunday _____
☐	☐	☐
☐	☐	☐
☐	☐	☐
☐	☐	☐
☐	☐	☐
☐	☐	☐
8		
9		
10		
11		
12		
1		
2		
3		
4		
5		
6		
7		

☐ _____
☐ _____
☐ _____
☐ _____
☐ _____
☐ _____
☐ _____

Weekly To-Do List

☐ _____
☐ _____
☐ _____
☐ _____
☐ _____
☐ _____
☐ _____
☐ _____
☐ _____
☐ _____
☐ _____

NOTES:

_____
_____
_____
_____
_____
_____

Weekly Affirmation: _____

_____
_____
_____
_____

Week of:_____

Priorities	Monday _____	Tuesday _____	Wednesday _____	Thursday _____
	☐	☐	☐	☐
	☐	☐	☐	☐
	☐	☐	☐	☐
	☐	☐	☐	☐
	☐	☐	☐	☐
	☐	☐	☐	☐
8				
9				
10				
11				
12				
1				
2				
3				
4				
5				
6				
7				

Number of Weekly Goals Reached:

_____Social Media Posts	_____Handed Out Business Cards	_____New Contracts
_____Calls	_____Appointments	_____Purchases
_____Talked to People	_____Listing Presentations	_____Rentals
_____New Contacts	_____Listings	_____Referrals

Month: _____

Friday _____	Saturday _____	Sunday _____
☐	☐	☐
☐	☐	☐
☐	☐	☐
☐	☐	☐
☐	☐	☐
☐	☐	☐
8		
9		
10		
11		
12		
1		
2		
3		
4		
5		
6		
7		

Weekly Goals

☐ _____
☐ _____
☐ _____
☐ _____
☐ _____
☐ _____
☐ _____

Weekly To-Do List

☐ _____
☐ _____
☐ _____
☐ _____
☐ _____
☐ _____
☐ _____
☐ _____
☐ _____
☐ _____

NOTES:

_____
_____
_____
_____
_____

Weekly Affirmation: _____

_____
_____
_____
_____

Week of:_____

Priorities	Monday _____	Tuesday _____	Wednesday _____	Thursday _____
	☐	☐	☐	☐
	☐	☐	☐	☐
	☐	☐	☐	☐
	☐	☐	☐	☐
	☐	☐	☐	☐
	☐	☐	☐	☐
8				
9				
10				
11				
12				
1				
2				
3				
4				
5				
6				
7				

Number of Weekly Goals Reached:

_____Social Media Posts   _____Handed Out Business Cards   _____New Contracts

_____Calls   _____Appointments   _____Purchases

_____Talked to People   _____Listing Presentations   _____Rentals

_____New Contacts   _____Listings   _____Referrals

Month: _____

Friday _____	Saturday _____	Sunday _____
☐	☐	☐
☐	☐	☐
☐	☐	☐
☐	☐	☐
☐	☐	☐
☐	☐	☐
8		
9		
10		
11		
12		
1		
2		
3		
4		
5		
6		
7		

Weekly Goals

☐ _____
☐ _____
☐ _____
☐ _____
☐ _____
☐ _____
☐ _____

Weekly To-Do List

☐ _____
☐ _____
☐ _____
☐ _____
☐ _____
☐ _____
☐ _____
☐ _____
☐ _____
☐ _____

NOTES:

_____
_____
_____
_____
_____
_____

Weekly Affirmation: _____

_____
_____
_____
_____

Approaches/Posts/Calls Goal Tracking

Start	1	2	3	4	5
	6	7	8	9	10
	11	12	13	14	15
	16	17	18	19	20
	21	22	23	24	25
	26	27	28	29	30
	31	32	33	34	35
	36	37	38	39	40
	41	42	43	44	45
Goal	46	47	48	49	50

Results:

_____

_____

_____

Monthly Realized Goals

☐ _____

☐ _____

☐ _____

☐ _____

☐ _____

☐ _____

☐ _____

☐ _____

☐ _____

What did you learn this month?

_____

_____

_____

_____

_____

_____

Notes:

_____

_____

_____

_____

_____

_____

_____

_____

_____

_____

_____

_____

_____

_____

_____

_____

_____

_____

_____

Month: _____

Monday	Tuesday	Wednesday	Thursday	Friday
☐	☐	☐	☐	☐
☐	☐	☐	☐	☐
☐	☐	☐	☐	☐
☐	☐	☐	☐	☐
☐	☐	☐	☐	☐

Number of Monthly Goals Reached:

_____Social Media Posts	_____Handed Out Business Cards	_____New Contracts
_____Calls	_____Appointments	_____Purchases
_____Talked to People	_____Listing Presentations	_____Rentals
_____New Contacts	_____Listings	_____Referrals

20_____

Monthly Goals

- ☐ _____
- ☐ _____
- ☐ _____
- ☐ _____
- ☐ _____
- ☐ _____

Saturday	Sunday
☐	☐
☐	☐
☐	☐
☐	☐
☐	☐

Monthly To-Do List

- ☐ _____
- ☐ _____
- ☐ _____
- ☐ _____
- ☐ _____
- ☐ _____
- ☐ _____
- ☐ _____
- ☐ _____
- ☐ _____

NOTES:

_____
_____
_____
_____
_____

Monthly Affirmation: _____

_____
_____
_____

Week of:_____

Monday _____	Tuesday _____	Wednesday _____	Thursday _____
☐	☐	☐	☐
☐	☐	☐	☐
☐	☐	☐	☐
☐	☐	☐	☐
☐	☐	☐	☐
☐	☐	☐	☐
8			
9			
10			
11			
12			
1			
2			
3			
4			
5			
6			
7			

Priorities

Number of Weekly Goals Reached:

_____Social Media Posts	_____Handed Out Business Cards	_____New Contracts
_____Calls	_____Appointments	_____Purchases
_____Talked to People	_____Listing Presentations	_____Rentals
_____New Contacts	_____Listings	_____Referrals

Month: _____

Weekly Goals

Friday _____	Saturday _____	Sunday _____
☐	☐	☐
☐	☐	☐
☐	☐	☐
☐	☐	☐
☐	☐	☐
☐	☐	☐
8		
9		
10		
11		
12		
1		
2		
3		
4		
5		
6		
7		

Weekly Goals
☐ _____
☐ _____
☐ _____
☐ _____
☐ _____
☐ _____
☐ _____

Weekly To-Do List

☐ _____
☐ _____
☐ _____
☐ _____
☐ _____
☐ _____
☐ _____
☐ _____
☐ _____

NOTES:

_____
_____
_____

Weekly Affirmation: _____

_____
_____
_____
_____
_____

Week of:_____

Priorities	Monday _____	Tuesday _____	Wednesday _____	Thursday _____
	☐	☐	☐	☐
	☐	☐	☐	☐
	☐	☐	☐	☐
	☐	☐	☐	☐
	☐	☐	☐	☐
	☐	☐	☐	☐
8				
9				
10				
11				
12				
1				
2				
3				
4				
5				
6				
7				

Number of Weekly Goals Reached:

_____Social Media Posts	_____Handed Out Business Cards	_____New Contracts
_____Calls	_____Appointments	_____Purchases
_____Talked to People	_____Listing Presentations	_____Rentals
_____New Contacts	_____Listings	_____Referrals

Month: _____

Weekly Goals

Friday _____	Saturday _____	Sunday _____
☐	☐	☐
☐	☐	☐
☐	☐	☐
☐	☐	☐
☐	☐	☐
☐	☐	☐
8		
9		
10		
11		
12		
1		
2		
3		
4		
5		
6		
7		

Weekly Goals

☐ _____
☐ _____
☐ _____
☐ _____
☐ _____
☐ _____
☐ _____
☐ _____

Weekly To-Do List

☐ _____
☐ _____
☐ _____
☐ _____
☐ _____
☐ _____
☐ _____
☐ _____
☐ _____
☐ _____

NOTES:

Weekly Affirmation: _____

Week of:____________________

	Monday _____	Tuesday _____	Wednesday _____	Thursday _____
Priorities	☐	☐	☐	☐
	☐	☐	☐	☐
	☐	☐	☐	☐
	☐	☐	☐	☐
	☐	☐	☐	☐
	☐	☐	☐	☐
	8			
	9			
	10			
	11			
	12			
	1			
	2			
	3			
	4			
	5			
	6			
	7			

Number of Weekly Goals Reached:

______Social Media Posts
______Handed Out Business Cards
______New Contracts

______Calls
______Appointments
______Purchases

______Talked to People
______Listing Presentations
______Rentals

______New Contacts
______Listings
______Referrals

Month: _____

Friday _____	Saturday _____	Sunday _____
☐	☐	☐
☐	☐	☐
☐	☐	☐
☐	☐	☐
☐	☐	☐
☐	☐	☐
8		
9		
10		
11		
12		
1		
2		
3		
4		
5		
6		
7		

Weekly Goals

☐ _____
☐ _____
☐ _____
☐ _____
☐ _____
☐ _____
☐

Weekly To-Do List

☐ _____
☐ _____
☐ _____
☐ _____
☐ _____
☐ _____
☐ _____
☐ _____
☐ _____
☐ _____

NOTES:

_____
_____
_____
_____
_____

Weekly Affirmation: _____

_____
_____
_____
_____

Week of:_____

Priorities	Monday _____	Tuesday _____	Wednesday _____	Thursday _____
	☐	☐	☐	☐
	☐	☐	☐	☐
	☐	☐	☐	☐
	☐	☐	☐	☐
	☐	☐	☐	☐
	☐	☐	☐	☐
8				
9				
10				
11				
12				
1				
2				
3				
4				
5				
6				
7				

Number of Weekly Goals Reached:

_____Social Media Posts	_____Handed Out Business Cards	_____New Contracts
_____Calls	_____Appointments	_____Purchases
_____Talked to People	_____Listing Presentations	_____Rentals
_____New Contacts	_____Listings	_____Referrals

Month: _____

Friday ____	Saturday ____	Sunday ____
☐	☐	☐
☐	☐	☐
☐	☐	☐
☐	☐	☐
☐	☐	☐
☐	☐	☐
8		
9		
10		
11		
12		
1		
2		
3		
4		
5		
6		
7		

Weekly Goals

☐ _____
☐ _____
☐ _____
☐ _____
☐ _____
☐ _____
☐ _____

Weekly To-Do List

☐ _____
☐ _____
☐ _____
☐ _____
☐ _____
☐ _____
☐ _____
☐ _____
☐ _____
☐ _____

NOTES:

_____
_____
_____
_____
_____
_____

Weekly Affirmation: _____

_____
_____
_____
_____

Week of:_____

Priorities	Monday _____	Tuesday _____	Wednesday _____	Thursday _____
	☐	☐	☐	☐
	☐	☐	☐	☐
	☐	☐	☐	☐
	☐	☐	☐	☐
	☐	☐	☐	☐
	☐	☐	☐	☐
8				
9				
10				
11				
12				
1				
2				
3				
4				
5				
6				
7				

Number of Weekly Goals Reached:

_____Social Media Posts	_____Handed Out Business Cards	_____New Contracts
_____Calls	_____Appointments	_____Purchases
_____Talked to People	_____Listing Presentations	_____Rentals
_____New Contacts	_____Listings	_____Referrals

Month: _____

Friday _____	Saturday _____	Sunday _____
☐	☐	☐
☐	☐	☐
☐	☐	☐
☐	☐	☐
☐	☐	☐
☐	☐	☐
8		
9		
10		
11		
12		
1		
2		
3		
4		
5		
6		
7		

Weekly Goals

☐ _____
☐ _____
☐ _____
☐ _____
☐ _____
☐ _____
☐ _____

Weekly To-Do List

☐ _____
☐ _____
☐ _____
☐ _____
☐ _____
☐ _____
☐ _____
☐ _____
☐ _____
☐ _____
☐ _____

NOTES:

_____
_____
_____
_____
_____

Weekly Affirmation: _____

_____
_____
_____
_____

Approaches/Posts/Calls Goal Tracking

Start 1	2	3	4	5
6	7	8	9	10
11	12	13	14	15
16	17	18	19	20
21	22	23	24	25
26	27	28	29	30
31	32	33	34	35
36	37	38	39	40
41	42	43	44	45
Goal 46	47	48	49	50

Monthly Realized Goals

☐ _____
☐ _____
☐ _____
☐ _____
☐ _____
☐ _____
☐ _____
☐ _____
☐ _____

What did you learn this month?

_____

_____

_____

_____

_____

_____

Results:

_____

_____

_____

Notes:

_____

_____

_____

_____

_____

_____

_____

_____

_____

_____

_____

_____

_____

_____

_____

_____

_____

_____

Operational Plan			
What to do? Objectives	How to do it? Activities	When to do it? Dates	With what resources?

Action Plan Activities

Specific objective	Activity	Strategies	Resources	Responsible	Date	Evaluation

Vision Board (Six Life Visions)

Vision Board (Life Vision Four Areas)

Vision Board (Personal and Business)

Vision Board (Career Only)

List of Tasks/To Do Lists

To Do	When	Priority

List of Tasks/To Do Lists

To Do	When	Priority

Important chapters to remember	Important pages to remember	Call script/pages to remember
		Buyer
		Seller
		FSBO
		Expired
		Short Sale
		Lessor
		Tenant
		Approach People
		Referred

Business Debut Timetable

Time	Activity	Sponsor	By:	Other

Raffle form

Welcome to the Business Debut of [Insert Logo]		
Guest Information		
Name:		
Phone:		
Email:		
Address:		
Referred by:		
Homeowner? YES ☐ NO ☐ Wanting to rent? Yes ☐ No ☐ Looking for service? YES ☐ NO ☐ Tell me how I can help:		
Receive a ticket for each referral you list. If you fill out all five referrals, you receive a gift!		
Name	Phone	Email
1.		
2.		
3.		
4.		
5.		

Ivania Alvarado

I believe in five universal values: God, myself, family, career, and positive pleasures. I am a licensed Real Estate broker and Real Estate Instructor. I have a certificate of Business Specialist-General Business, among other studies and certificates. I graduated from Supervision and Management–Accounting Concentration from one of the biggest community colleges in the United States, Miami Dade College. I am also a student at Florida Atlantic University studying a Master of Taxation with a graduation date of December 2022. Since 1995, I have been involved in various real estate businesses including real estate sales, insurance, title companies, and a real estate school starting in 1999. The school introduced me to writing when I created the *Real Estate Manual*. This manual formed a fundamental basis for training seminars in this profession. I have had extensive experience in education and promoting salespeople by recruiting, training, advising, and educating. South Florida School of Real Estate (SFSRE.NET) has graduated more than a thousand students.

In 2001, I started writing again, contributing the "Los sueños y Usted" (Your Dreams and You) section in various magazines. That led to me writing the book *Los Sueños y Usted*. In 2004, I was inspired to create a musical CD, composed with great care and dedication, called *Los Sueños y Usted*, which became a radio and television program. In 2016, I rewrote *Los Sueños y Usted* and translated the book into English as *Your Dreams and You*. In 2021, I expanded *Your Dreams and You* into a journal and planner available in both English and Spanish, and in paperback and hardback. They are available on Amazon.com. Visit IvaniaAlvarado.com for more information.

My most spiritually lucrative achievements are the help I give to religious institutions to help the homeless, Mother Teresa of Calcutta's community of the old, sick, and addicted.

Please visit the following websites for more information about my real estate journey. Thank you for your time in reading this manual and for your interest in real estate. I look forward to meeting you, working together, and leading you into the world of real estate.

www.sfsre.net

www.IvaniaAlvarado.com